New Directions for Adult and Continuing Education

Susan Imel
Jovita M. Ross-Gordon
COEDITORS-IN-CHIEF

Meeting the Transitional Needs of Young Adult Learners

C. Amelia Davis
Joann S. Olson
EDITORS

Number 143 • Fall 2014
Jossey-Bass
San Francisco

Meeting the Transitional Needs of Young Adult Learners
C. Amelia Davis, Joann S. Olson (eds)
New Directions for Adult and Continuing Education, no. 143
Susan Imel, Jovita M. Ross-Gordon, Coeditors-in-Chief

Microfilm copies of issues and articles are available in 16mm and 35mm, as well as microfiche in 105mm, through University Microfilms Inc., 300 North Zeeb Road, Ann Arbor, Michigan 48106-1346.

New Directions for Adult and Continuing Education (ISSN 1052-2891, electronic ISSN 1536-0717) is part of The Jossey-Bass Higher and Adult Education Series and is published quarterly by Wiley Subscription Services, Inc., A Wiley Company, at Jossey-Bass, One Montgomery Street, Suite 1200, San Francisco, CA 94104-4594. POSTMASTER: Send address changes to New Directions for Adult and Continuing Education, Jossey-Bass, One Montgomery Street, Suite 1200, San Francisco, CA 94104-4594.

New Directions for Adult and Continuing Education is indexed in CIJE: Current Index to Journals in Education (ERIC); Contents Pages in Education (T&F); ERIC Database (Education Resources Information Center); Higher Education Abstracts (Claremont Graduate University); and Sociological Abstracts (CSA/CIG).

Individual subscription rate (in USD): $89 per year US/Can/Mex, $113 rest of world; institutional subscription rate: $311 US, $351 Can/Mex, $385 rest of world. Single copy rate: $29. Electronic only–all regions: $89 individual, $311 institutional; Print & Electronic–US: $98 individual, $357 institutional; Print & Electronic–Canada/Mexico: $98 individual, $397 institutional; Print & Electronic–Rest of World: $122 individual, $431 institutional.

Editorial correspondence should be sent to the Coeditors-in-Chief, Susan Imel, 3076 Woodbine Place, Columbus, Ohio 43202-1341, e-mail: imel.l@osu.edu; or Jovita M. Ross-Gordon, Southwest Texas State University, CLAS Dept., 601 University Drive, San Marcos, TX 78666.

Cover photograph by Jack Hollingsworth@Photodisc

www.josseybass.com

Contents

Editors' Notes

The word transition conveys movement, leaving one thing behind and becoming something else. The caterpillar becomes a butterfly after metamorphosis. With a twist of the wrist, the image at the end of the kaleidoscope changes. For many, graduation from high school seemingly marks the transition from student to something else. Transition begets change, and something new emerges.

And yet, even these examples suggest that looking closely at any particular transition reveals it as more complex than it first seemed. If the caterpillar has two states of being—caterpillar and butterfly—then what is to be made of the time in the chrysalis? The kaleidoscope can produce a seemingly infinite number of patterns. And new graduates are often surprised to discover just how much they still don't know. Transitions often do not have clearly defined beginnings or endings, and they can be disruptive. Given the comprehensive nature of many of life's transitions, what is the role of the educator in helping others navigate transition? More precisely to the point of this volume: What are the transitional and educational needs of young adults as they transition to adulthood?

There has not been a *New Directions for Adult and Continuing Education* sourcebook related to young adult learners since Darkenwald and Knox (1984) edited *Meeting Educational Needs of Young Adults*. As the editors stated then, young adults are an important segment of the adult population but have received scant attention in the adult education literature.

Increasingly, youths and young adults are enrolling in adult education programs and in doing so are changing the meaning of adulthood. Given the significant demographic, technological, and cultural shifts during the past 30 years, there is an increasing need for practitioners and program planners to reconsider what constitutes "adult" and "adult education." An understanding of the changing meaning of adulthood is fundamental to developing programs and policies that will address the needs of younger learners, and we believe it is time for an updated discussion among adult educators and scholars in other disciplines. This volume is designed to reignite the discussion related to meeting the educational needs of young adults along with a timely and interdisciplinary discussion that highlights the transitional needs of young adult learners.

In Chapter 1 of this volume, Johanna Wyn challenges a simplistic understanding of "transition" and "adulthood." She suggests that a focus on transition is steeped in linear theories of psychology and human development that rely on normative—and perhaps outdated—understandings of the markers of adulthood. As an alternative, she proposes that a metaphor of "belonging," rather than "transition," more accurately describes this time of life, as young adults understand their present reality and begin to conceptualize their future possibilities in the context of the quality of their relationships and connections.

Brendaly Drayton explores the intersection of cultural identity, social conditions, and the transition to adulthood in Chapter 2. Using a critical sociocultural perspective, she illustrates how culture orients developmental tasks and learning for emerging adults from dominant and minority cultures. Strategies for developing cultural competency and implications for adult education are discussed.

The transitional needs of vulnerable youth are highlighted by Rongbing Xie, Bisakha (Pia) Sen, and E. Michael Foster in Chapter 3. For many of these vulnerable youth, their relationship with the systems they have engaged with or relied on—mental health and social service agencies, the foster care system, or criminal justice systems—ends abruptly when they reach the age of majority. Xie et al. explore the impact of those individual histories on the process and experience of transitioning to adulthood.

Chapter 4, written by Jessica Nina Lester, focuses on how youth with dis/ability labels navigate the meaning and markers of adulthood. She outlines several of the policies designed to support these young adults, while at the same time suggesting that little research has been conducted related to how individuals, educators, and employers have responded to these policies and mandates. Furthermore, she explores the implications of reframing dis/ability labels as a social construct, suggesting that this approach may help adult educators who wish to support young adults with dis/ability labels in a meaningful way.

Recognizing that an individual's various affiliations may influence his or her sense of self and adulthood, Chapter 5 presents an exploration of the transition to adulthood in communities of faith, written by Steven B. Frye. Many young adults are disengaging from the faith communities of their childhood, leaving many congregations wondering about long-term survival and vitality. The key elements of engaging young adults in faith communities in more meaningful ways—community, authenticity, experience, and so on—may also prove effective in a variety of adult education settings.

As described by C. Amelia Davis in Chapter 6, recent demographic shifts within Adult Basic Education/GED programs have the potential to significantly change the work of adult educators in these programs. The purpose of this chapter is to consider alternative ways of thinking about transitions to adulthood through the context of youths transitioning as adult learners. Drawing on findings from a recent narrative study in which 18- to 25-year-old GED students shared their experiences transitioning from high school to adult education, Davis discusses the potential implications these transitions have on program planning and policy in adult education.

Preparing young adults for workplace and nonformal learning, as they move from formalized school settings, is the focus of Joann S. Olson's discussion, found in Chapter 7. She outlines how this aspect of the transition to adulthood may be experienced by recent graduates, including several

New Directions for Adult and Continuing Education • DOI: 10.1002/ace

challenges perhaps particularly salient to first-generation college graduates. Her chapter highlights strategies for both school-based and workplace educators that may help prepare young adults develop the skill and attitude of lifelong learning.

Chapter 8 outlines several themes that infuse the chapters of this volume. It is our hope that as you engage with the ideas here you will be reminded— as we were—of the necessity of our work as adult educators. Supporting young adults during this time of life is a complex endeavor, requiring nuanced and thoughtful approaches. The challenge of the task speaks to its great importance.

C. Amelia Davis
Joann S. Olson
Editors

Reference

Darkenwald, G. G., & Knox, A. B. (Eds.). (1984). *New Directions for Adult and Continuing Education: No. 21. Meeting educational needs of young adults.* San Francisco, CA: Jossey-Bass.

C. AMELIA DAVIS *is an assistant professor of educational research in the Department of Curriculum, Foundations, and Reading in the College of Education at Georgia Southern University.*

JOANN S. OLSON *is an assistant professor and program coordinator in the adult and higher education program at the University of Houston-Victoria.*

1

This chapter provides an overview of theories of the transition to young adulthood. It sets out the argument for conceptual renewal and discusses some implications of new patterns of transition for adult education.

Conceptualizing Transitions to Adulthood

Johanna Wyn

In the fields of adult education and youth studies, thinking around the concepts of youth, young adults, and the nature of adulthood has been undergoing a transformation, reflecting changes in the ways in which people are living and learning in the 21st century.[1] In this chapter, I set out the arguments for conceptual renewal, drawing on insights about youth and adult development from the fields of youth studies and education, through a consideration of (a) a brief history and analysis of current debates in youth transitions research, (b) the social conditions that have forged a "new adulthood," and (c) the challenges that these conditions place on the traditional metaphor of youth to adult transitions. Finally, I discuss the implications of these considerations for adult learning.

There is a comprehensive body of work that documents and analyzes the generational shift between the baby boomer generation and subsequent generations (often referred to as Generations X and Y). Although there is debate about the exact nature of these changes and their implications, there is an emerging consensus that the social transformations that occurred during the 1980s and 1990s in Western countries have changed the nature of youth and adulthood, with significant implications for how young adults work, live, and learn. This chapter discusses how a range of theorists have understood these changes to youth transitions. The blurring of the boundaries between youth and adulthood has led to a body of work that interrogates how disciplines such as developmental psychology and sociology have constructed truths and naturalized ways of thinking about young people. I discuss these arguments and some of the developments that are emerging from those arguments.

The Idea of Youth Transitions and the New Adulthood

The idea of youth transitions has played a significant role in youth studies and youth policy, especially since the 1980s, when youth labor markets in developed countries began to fail. As full-time employment and career opportunities

New Directions for Adult and Continuing Education, no. 143, Fall 2014 © 2014 Wiley Periodicals, Inc.
Published online in Wiley Online Library (wileyonlinelibrary.com) • DOI: 10.1002/ace.20100

for young people in economies based on manufacturing and primary industries have become increasingly scarce (ILO, 2013), education has become both a refuge from unemployment and a ticket to employment in emerging knowledge, service, and high-skill economies (Furlong, 2013). As a result, youth transitions to adulthood were characterized as *extended* (Furlong & Cartmel, 2007) and *arrested* (Côté, 2000) toward an *emerging* but ever-retreating state of adulthood (Bynner, 2005). These analyses sought to understand new patterns of transition from youth to adulthood as the patterns that characterized the baby boomer generation (born between 1946 and 1965) were superseded. Generation X (born between 1965 and 1976) became the pioneers of new patterns of transition that have largely been replicated by Generation Y (born between 1977 and 2001). Although these definitions of generations are not particularly scientific, most analyses of shifts in generational patterns of transition conform broadly to this schema. For example, the socioeconomic changes of the late 1980s through the 2000s and the generational differences that resulted are noted in a range of work on "new adulthoods" and generational effects in France (Chauvel, 2010), Italy (Leccardi, 2012), Australia and Canada (Andres & Wyn, 2010), in the United States (Gerson, 2010), and across many other countries (Esping-Andersen, 2009).

For young adults aged 19–25, global changes in the nature of production and labor markets were reflected in an increase in the time spent in formal education and a decrease in full-time, secure labor market participation. In turn, these developments have resulted in increased financial dependency on parents or welfare, increased levels of financial debt for the young (Schneider, 2000), and later marriage for both men and women compared with the previous generation (Esping-Andersen, 2009).

The phrase "new adulthood" describes the implications of altered circumstances for young people's options (Wyn, Smith, Stokes, Tyler, & Woodman, 2008). The combination of education and labor market conditions referred to above have, for a majority of young adults, foreclosed some options like achieving financial independence in their early twenties and opened up other opportunities such as taking one or more gap years, living in group households, or undertaking education outside of one's home country. New communication technologies have widened the scope of opportunities that young adults see for themselves and created global connections around leisure, employment, and education that bring new imagined futures (Rizvi, 2012). These developments have led to the proliferation of diverse experiences of youth and complex trajectories alongside recognized markers of progress.

The patterns of life that characterize the new adulthood have also been accompanied by shifts in disposition. For example, the *Life Patterns* study (Andres & Wyn, 2010; Cuervo & Wyn, 2012) showed how the increase in educational participation by young people in the 1990s was accompanied by a widespread belief in the inherent value of investing in educational credentials. Education was seen as a way of securing a foothold in an increasingly complex and precarious labor market. This theme has been taken up by Brown, Lauder, and Ashton (2011) who analyze how the investment in education by individuals has not been matched by the other part of the "neoliberal bargain"—the promise of jobs and rewards. They argue that the global financial crisis of the mid-2000s has underlined the failure of many national economies, from Greece to the United Kingdom, from New Zealand to the United States, to deliver high-skill, secure, and well-paid jobs for graduates.

In addition, many youth researchers have drawn on the individualization thesis outlined by Beck and Beck-Gernsheim (2002) and Bauman (2001) that young people have responded to the complexity and uncertainty of the education–job nexus (or transition) by (a) taking individual responsibility for the failures of economic systems to generate stable employment opportunities and (b) engaging in intensive identity work that enables them to respond flexibly to changing conditions. This involves developing a capacity to hold options open, to invest in networks and connections that enable them to gain an understanding of different work identities, and to work on the self as a project, reflexively viewing themselves as others might do (Woodman & Wyn, 2011). These responses have often led to characterizing members of Generation X as having stalled lives or as having entered an extended adolescence, reflecting concern that this generation was not "settling down" as the previous generation had (Côté & Allahar, 1996).

During the 1950s and 1960s, a range of theorists including Piaget (1954) and Erikson (1965) expanded on Hall's ideas of adolescent development, drawing on social–biological and structural–functionalist concepts (Hall, 1904). As Jones (2009) explains, these theories built on Freud's notion of the developmental stages of the psyche from infancy to maturity to propose that youth represented a stage of life during which developmental tasks must be mastered to ensure healthy, rational adulthood.

At around the same time, theories about the creation of deviant and resistant youth cultures and subcultures with distinctive styles and social practices emerged (Coleman, 1961; Reich, 1972): The Centre for Contemporary Cultural Studies (CCCS) at the University of Birmingham took up this focus during the 1970s (Hall & Jefferson, 1976). The early work of the CCCS represented a shift from deviant or spectacular cultural manifestations toward a sociological understanding of how working-class young people unconsciously contribute to the reproduction of social inequalities through peer-based cultures of resistance that reinforce rather than challenge existing power relations (Willis, 1977).

The youth transitions approach that came into vogue in the 1980s, however, tended to take cultural expression for granted, drawing implicitly on developmental approaches to identify a sociological progression through institutional stages such as education, employment, marriage, and independent living. This focus on trajectories through institutional and social markers of progress contributed to a division between transitions and cultural approaches in the field of youth studies that has persisted to the present (Cohen & Ainley, 2000; Furlong, Woodman, & Wyn, 2011). An alignment between developmental and transitions approaches is evident in the way that both rest on the idea of normative transitional stages, drawing on categories of mainstream and at-risk and assuming an (essentialist) adult status as the endpoint of the trajectory. As Talburt and Lesko (2012) pointed out, "youth" invokes a universal category of transitional beings on their way to productive, responsible, and legal adulthood (p. 2).

Over time, a body of work that is critical of elements of a transitions approach has developed. While it is neither possible nor desirable to characterize all of the youth research that draws on a transitions metaphor neatly, it is important to acknowledge the criticism that linear transitions through set markers and stages have become reified through frameworks of measurement (France, 2007; Wyn, Lantz, & Harris, 2012). France (2007) argued that the reliance on normative patterns of transition has the effect of creating nonconforming or "at-risk" categories of youth who become the targets of policy interventions aimed at creating conformity. This approach to closing the "gaps" between conforming and nonconforming, or successful and failing, young people has been criticized for its failure to acknowledge the conditions that create inequalities and marginalization, particularly by educators (Hayes, 2012; Lingard, 2011). Others have drawn attention to the ways in which practices of governance, based on definitions of deserving and undeserving youth, constitute categories of youth (Kelly, 2006; Mizen, 2004). The conflation of youth, and adulthood, with age categories has been criticized by Lesko (1996) and, more recently, Blatterer (2007). These researchers point out that the nature and meanings of youth and of adulthood are determined by social conditions and relationships, not by biology. Both reflect on the way that youth is "book-ended" by an uncritical concept of adulthood as a point of arrival.

Drawing on these critiques, Furlong et al. (2011) have argued that it is timely to consider the synergies between cultural and transitional approaches to youth studies. This argument calls for research focusing on young people's trajectories to give greater recognition to the situated, cultural, and relational aspects of young people's lives, while also recognizing institutional processes of progression. Against a backdrop of significant social and economic change over the last quarter of a century, young people have forged new transition patterns through new ways of managing their life contexts, drawing on the search for meaning and security in an unpredictable and unstable world. The convergence between cultural and transitional strands of youth research recognizes young people's subjectivities as well as their transition patterns. As Ball (2006) argued, it is important for researchers to acknowledge how the frameworks we use constitute the subjects of research. Talburt and Lesko (2012) pointed out that young people are known, and youth is constructed, "through a historical process of shifting assemblages of rationalities, technologies, practices, institutions, and individuals" (p. 5). The point is to interrogate the logics that these processes create and to resist embedding orthodoxies.

New Directions for Adult and Continuing Education • DOI: 10.1002/ace

Rethinking the Transitions Metaphor

Although the idea of youth transitions remains central to youth studies—especially to policy-related research—there is an emerging consensus that this spatial concept of youth may need to be expanded, or that a different metaphor might be needed, to take full account of the young people's lives in the present and to acknowledge the qualities of relationships that enable young people to be productively connected to their worlds. In order to fully theorize age as a social relation, and to understand how the nature and quality of connections with people, resources, and places contribute to young people's quality of life, a relational approach is needed. To put this more explicitly, the developmental foundations of the metaphor of transitions, as applied to youth studies, position youth as a stage, phase, and space through which ideal trajectories to adulthood may be forged. A metaphor of belonging focuses on the quality of connections and relationship forged by young people and enabled by institutional processes that constitute what is possible for youth.

Relational Frameworks. The field of youth studies contains many examples of research that employs a relational framework. For example, the *Inventing Adulthoods* study explored the changing nature of adulthood in the United Kingdom in the early 2000s (Henderson et al., 2007). This study, based on longitudinal research, analyzes how young people seek out ways to be competent and achieve recognition in different areas of their lives including education, employment, family, and civic life. More importantly, this research highlights the active work that young people do belong. The *Life Patterns* study of Generation X in Australia and Canada has analyzed how a new adulthood was forged by young people as they navigated the new economic realities of the 1990s and found new ways to be connected meaningfully to institutions, people, and places (Andres & Wyn, 2010; Cuervo & Wyn, 2012). The sense that new patterns of life are being created through these active processes of navigation by young people is evident in the collection of research on a "new youth" by Leccardi and Ruspini (2006). Leccardi's (2012) work explored new temporalities of life among young people in Italy as they grapple with unpredictability and the impossibility of imagining the future that was constructed by the baby boomer generation; this theme was also taken up by Woodman (2012) who explored the issue of temporality in the lives of young Australians during their immediate postschool years. These authors look between the spaces of transition markers, as Hall, Coffey, and Lashua (2009) suggested, to understand how the fragmentation of life that is associated with precarious work, combined with complex educational timetables, has resulted in the acceleration of temporal norms and expectations, which undermines the conditions for maintaining strong personal connections.

Belonging. The idea of belonging is implicit in much of the research that contributes to youth studies. This includes research that focuses on the synergies between youth cultures and transitions research (Furlong et al.,

2011), on the intersections between locality and biography (Kraack & Kenway, 2002), and on struggles for identity (Stokes, 2012). Belonging is a descriptive term that invites the researcher and policy maker to map and understand how young people put together the complex elements of life that enable them to be connected, to be included, to be healthy, to participate, and to be economically stable (Tilleczek, 2010). This approach opens up an understanding of the resources including family, friends, education, and peers that young people draw on to build their lives and the ways in which changing conditions impact life chances. Hall et al. (2009) showed how narratives of transformation redevelopment and regeneration of a rural community interact with young people's biographical transformations. This work identified the importance of understanding the connections between young people and place.

As these studies demonstrate, alongside the metaphor of transitions with its focus on markers and stages of progress, more explicit frameworks are needed that enable researchers to integrate economic change (i.e., school to work) with other dimensions of life, including well-being and relationships with people and place. A metaphor of belonging encompasses these elements.

For the current generation, more needs to be known about how decisions about education and employment are made in relation to belonging—socially, geographically, and economically. Understanding the relationships between education and employment in context is especially important in times of increased economic insecurity, precisely because the links between education and employment are less reliable. The following section argues that it is timely to draw on conceptual frameworks that view education as a strategy and a relationship—not a transition space—in the struggle to construct a life.

The challenge for all educators, and especially for adult educators, is that the reality of people's lives is multidimensional, messy, and almost always non-linear. A transitions approach that focuses on the school–work nexus obscures other significant areas that influence learning, such as well-being, relationships with people and place, the environment, and leisure.

Young Adults and Learning

Considerations of social change and conceptual renewal have implications for all educators, including those who focus on adult education. Young people are quick to respond to new circumstances, mainly because they have to. Institutions are often the slowest to respond, in part because they bear the imprint of their origins. Young adults in the 21st century require education that takes a flexible approach to age, education that recognizes diverse needs as well as young adults' capacity to make decisions and take responsibility for their learning. Active engagement in decision making, flexible approaches to the relationship between age and learning, and creative learning environments that

New Directions for Adult and Continuing Education • DOI: 10.1002/ace

meet diverse needs are important elements that help to equip young people to be effective navigators of their own lives and participants in creating an economically sustainable society.

Adult education has a heightened significance in a context of economic uncertainty and global competition for high-skill jobs. The nexus between education and employment is not robust, and there is increasing evidence that the value of education in globalized labor markets is being driven down, and a new category of "overeducated" individuals is being created (Brown et al., 2011; ILO, 2013). Nonetheless, individuals without educational credentials tend to fare the worst in labor markets (ILO, 2013; OECD, 2007). These developments place even greater pressure on young people to be active decision makers who are also flexible and capable of navigating uncertainty. But, perhaps most importantly, they speak to the need for a new metaphor of education that enables educators to acknowledge education as a place of connection, where the quality of relationships is made visible, moving beyond the rather instrumental metaphor of education as a space of transition.

Connected, Locally and Globally. In changing social, economic, and political landscapes, education is shifting from being primarily a tool for economic advancement toward a wider societal role contributing to capacities to navigate complexity and to contribute to a sustainable society. Education is about the production of ways of being and knowing, as well as sets of skills and areas of knowledge. In a context in which young adults feel individual responsibility for the complex navigations and decision making that characterize their lives, responsibility for learning is shifting from the educator to the educated. This approach has been central to the work of adult educators for many years; moving the understanding of the "transition" to adulthood away from age-based or stage-based definitions toward ideas of belonging and connection, as described earlier, may also serve to blur the boundary between the roles of student and teacher. How young people learn in formal education settings can and should more closely approximate the way they learn outside of formal institutions, developing the capacities to understand what is relevant, how to access information, how to learn, and how to develop knowledge (see Olson, Chapter 7 of this volume).

Educational systems in many countries have been slow to respond to changes in young people's learning needs. Indeed some developments in education, focusing on internal processes such as "quality of teaching" and standardized tests, separate learning from broader social trends, emphasizing an abstract notion of student and a narrow notion of (academic) outcomes. This separation of schools from communities and their global context limits opportunities to make learning relevant, locally as well as globally, and can reinforce a view that "disadvantaged communities" have nothing positive to offer education.

Changing circumstances challenge educationalists to recognize the diversity of young adulthood and to understand and respond to the impact of different economic, political, and social environments on learning. As Bottrell and Goodwin (2011) noted in relation to Australian schools, "it appears that the role of schools in society may be changing, as new understandings of the relationships between the state, institutions, communities, families and individuals emerge" (p. 1).

Needs (Not Age) Based. The reliance on age as a key organizing principle reinforces a normative approach to learning and disconnects that learning from the context and circumstances of individuals and communities. Although significant advances have been made, educational systems still reflect the age-based nature of their origins in the 1950s. Early school leavers (or "dropouts") in particular find themselves shut out because, having left school, it can be difficult to reconnect with formal education (see Davis, Chapter 6 of this volume). New models of second-chance education are responding to this challenge, recognizing that age is an artificial barrier to learning and creating stronger articulation between different institutional sites of learning (e.g., between schools and "adult" learning institutions or between academic and "vocational" programs; Bottrell & Goodwin, 2011; te Riele, 2007).

Navigating Learning. Being "self-navigators" is increasingly necessary, in part because the links between education and employment are so complex. Research shows that educational qualifications, although important, do not correspond directly to employment outcomes (Andres & Wyn, 2010; Cuervo & Wyn, 2012). Young people do not necessarily expect to take up employment in their field of training, or they may seek work in that field for a short period of time only, exploring options to retrain in order to enter different fields of work. Being good navigators requires a conscious approach to personal development so that individuals can see how their personal biography has developed in the past and how it is currently being constructed so that they can make decisions about their future options. Being good navigators also requires a deep understanding of the nature of the social, economic, and political world in which they are living and their relationships with others, locally and globally. An example can be found in Wierenga and Guevara's (2013) analysis of a partnership between an international NGO and educational institutions in Australia and Indonesia that created adult learning opportunities that were also connected with secondary school–aged learning through peer-based citizenship education.

The focus on effective navigation has the capacity to address the needs of those who are currently most disadvantaged within education, who tend to be young people from low socioeconomic backgrounds, young indigenous people, and young people from rural areas. Already many educational programs consciously connect learning to place and build relationships across secondary and adult learning sites both locally and globally (Smyth, Angus,

Down, & McInerney, 2008). These programs explore local histories, linking local stories and experiences across different places and recognizing the skills that parents and community members can offer schools (Thomson & Harris, 2004).

Conclusions

An analysis of the idea of youth transitions provides fertile ground for adult educators. This chapter provides a historical perspective on youth development and youth transitions that aims to provoke reflection on the truths that are produced through commonly used theoretical frameworks of this transition. This chapter has explored the ways in which understandings of youth are naturalized and so become taken for granted. The focus of the chapter is on the complex relationship between social, economic, and political conditions and the nature and quality of young people's lives. These considerations are presented as a challenge and an opportunity for educational policy and for educators.

This chapter has argued that the idea of youth transitions is underpinned by a developmental/transitional metaphor linking psychological theories of youth development relatively seamlessly with sociological markers of progress through phases of the life cycle. While these approaches have the capacity to reveal important insights for adult educators about young people's lives today, there are inherent weaknesses in this approach, which it may be timely to address.

The reality of new transnational educational and labor market systems means that the nexus between education and employment, the mainstay of contemporary youth transitions approaches, is weak. Education manifestly no longer guarantees a smooth transition into secure employment, and educational policy based on monitoring transitional processes is less and less capable of delivering policy and programs that can address key issues of inequality of outcomes, much like adult basic, GED, and vocational education programs. Drawing on a body of work that critiques transitional approaches to youth, this chapter argues that a relational metaphor that places an emphasis on the quality and nature of connection and relationship provides a richer framework for understanding young people's lives and the role of education in their lives. Such a framework invites adult educators to be informed about who their students are and what their aspirations are. Adult education is a complex learning space that is traditionally associated with the acquisition of specific vocational skills. In these times, adult education is also a significant resource for young people's identity development that enables them to be connected, to be healthy, to participate and work.

Note

1. I draw on a sociological approach that acknowledges that youth is categorized in different ways across time and place. A survey of the age ranges that are included within

the category of youth reveals that this is a broad inclusive category that commonly begins at age 12 and continues to age 25, but there is considerable variation across policy areas and between countries (see Cuervo & Wyn, 2012). I use the words young people to refer to individuals and groups who are subject to this categorization. Because the range of ages that encompasses youth is extremely broad, I tend to use the term young people when referring to people aged 12–18 and use the term young adults when referring to youth aged from 19 to the late twenties.

References

Andres, L., & Wyn, J. (2010). *The making of a generation: The children of the 1970s in adulthood*. Toronto, Canada: University of Toronto Press.

Ball, S. (2006). The necessity and violence of theory. *Discourse: Studies in the Cultural Politics of Education, 27*(1), 3–10.

Bauman, Z. (2001). *The individualized society*. Cambridge, UK: Polity Press.

Beck, U., & Beck-Gernsheim, E. (2002). *Individualization*. London, UK: Sage.

Blatterer, H. (2007). *Coming of age in times of uncertainty*. New York, NY: Berghahn Books.

Bottrell, D., & Goodwin, S. (2011). Contextualising schools and communities. In D. Bottrell & S. Goodwin (Eds.), *Schools, communities and social inclusion* (pp. 1–20). Sydney, Australia: Palgrave/MacMillan.

Brown, P., Lauder, H., & Ashton, D. (2011). *The global auction: The broken promises of education, jobs and incomes*. New York, NY: Oxford University Press.

Bynner, J. (2005). Rethinking the youth phase of the life-course: The case for emerging adulthood? *Journal of Youth Studies, 8*(4), 367–384.

Chauvel, L. (2010). The long-term destabilization of youth, scarring effects, and the future of the welfare regime in post-Trente glorieuses France. *French Politics, Culture & Society, 28*(3), 74–96.

Cohen, P., & Ainley, P. (2000). In the country of the blind?: Youth studies and cultural studies in Britain. *Journal of Youth Studies, 3*(1), 79–95.

Coleman, J. (1961). *The adolescent society: The social life of the teenager and its impact on education*. New York, NY: Free Press of Glencoe.

Côté, J. (2000). *Arrested adulthood: The changing nature of maturity and identity*. New York: New York University Press.

Côté, J., & Allahar, A. (1996). *Generation on hold: Coming of age in the late twentieth century*. New York: New York University Press.

Cuervo, H., & Wyn, J. (2012). *Young people making it work: Continuity and change in rural places*. Melbourne, Australia: Melbourne University Publishing.

Erikson, E. H. (1965). *Childhood and society*. Harmondsworth, UK: Penguin Books.

Esping-Andersen, G. (2009). *The incomplete revolution: Adapting welfare states to women's new roles*. Oxford, UK: Polity Press.

France, A. (2007). *Understanding youth in late modernity*. Maidenhead, UK: Open University Press.

Furlong, A. (2013). *Youth studies: An introduction*. New York, NY: Routledge.

Furlong, A., & Cartmel, F. (2007). *Young people and social change*. Buckingham, UK: Open University Press.

Furlong, A., Woodman, D., & Wyn, J. (2011). Changing times, changing perspectives: Reconciling 'transition' and 'cultural' perspectives on youth and young adulthood. *Journal of Sociology, 47*(4), 355–370.

Gerson, K. (2010). *The unfinished revolution*. New York, NY: Oxford University Press.

Hall, G. S. (1904). *Adolescence*. New York, NY: Appleton.

Hall, S., & Jefferson, T. (Eds). (1976). *Resistance through rituals*. London, UK: Hutchinson.

Hall, T., Coffey, A., & Lashua, B. (2009). Steps and stages: Rethinking transitions in youth and place. *Journal of Youth Studies, 12*(5), 547–561.

Hayes, D. (2012). Re-engaging marginalised young people in learning: The contribution of informal learning and community-based collaborations. *Journal of Education Policy, 27*(5), 641–653.

Henderson, S., Holland, J., McGrellis, S., Sharpe, S., Thomson, R., & Grigoriou, T. (2007). *Inventing adulthoods: A biographical approach to youth transitions.* London, UK: Sage.

International Labour Organization (ILO). (2013). *Global employment trends for youth 2013: A crisis for youth.* Geneva, Switzerland: Author.

Jones, G. (2009). *Youth.* Cambridge, UK: Policy Press.

Kelly, P. (2006). The entrepreneurial self and "youth at-risk": Exploring the horizons of identity in the twenty-first century. *Journal of Youth Studies, 9*(1), 17–32.

Kraack, A., & Kenway, J. (2002). Place, time and stigmatised youthful identities: Bad boys in paradise. *Journal of Rural Studies, 18*, 145–55.

Leccardi, C. (2012). Young people's representations of the future and the acceleration of time: A generational approach. *Diskurs Kindheits-und Jungenforschung Heft, 7*(1), 59–73.

Leccardi, C., & Ruspini, E. (Eds.). (2006). *New youth? Young people, generations and family life.* Aldershot, UK: Ashgate.

Lesko, N. (1996). Denaturalizing adolescence: The politics of contemporary representations. *Youth & Society, 28*(2), 139–161.

Lingard, B. (2011). Policy as numbers: Ac/counting for research. *Australian Educational Researcher, 38*, 355–382.

Mizen, P. (2004). *The changing state of youth.* New York, NY: Palgrave.

Organization for Economic Cooperation and Development (OECD). (2007). *Higher education and regions: Globally competitive, locally engaged.* Paris, France: Author.

Piaget, J. (1954). *The construction of reality in the child.* New York, NY: Basic Books.

Reich, W. (1972). *The greening of America.* Harmondsworth, UK: Penguin.

Rizvi, F. (2012). Mobilities and the transnationalization of youth cultures. In N. Lesko & S. Talburt (Eds.), *Keywords in youth studies: Tracing affects, movements, knowledges* (pp. 191–202). New York, NY: Routledge.

Schneider, J. (2000). The increasing financial dependency of young people on their parents. *Journal of Youth Studies, 3*(1), 5–20.

Smyth, J., Angus, L., Down, B., & McInerney, P. (2008). *Critically engaged learning: Connecting to young lives.* New York, NY: Peter Lang.

Stokes, H. (2012). *Imagining futures: Identity narratives and the role of part time work, family and community.* Melbourne, Australia: Melbourne University Press.

Talburt, S., & Lesko, N. (2012). An introduction to seven technologies of youth studies. In N. Lesko & S. Talburt (Eds.), *Keywords in youth studies: Tracing affects, movements, knowledges* (pp. 1–10). New York, NY: Routledge.

te Riele, K. (2007). Educational alternatives for marginalised youth. *The Australian Educational Researcher, 34*(3), 53–68.

Thomson, P., & Harris, A. (2004, April). *Leading schools that serve neighbourhoods and communities in poverty.* Paper prepared for the Second International Leadership in Education Research Network Meeting, Boston, MA.

Tilleczek, K. (2010). *Approaching youth studies: Being, becoming and belonging.* Toronto, Canada: Oxford University Press.

Wierenga, A., & Guevara, R. (2013). *Local connections and global citizenship: A youth-led approach to learning and partnership.* Melbourne, Australia: Melbourne University Press.

Willis, P. (1977). *Learning to labour: How working class kids get working class jobs.* Farnbrough, UK: Saxon House.

Woodman, D. (2012). Life out of synch: How new patterns of further education and the rise of precarious employment are reshaping young people's relationships. *Sociology, 46*(6), 1074–1090.

Woodman, D., & Wyn, J. (2011). Youth research in a changing world. In S. Beadle, R. Holdsworth, & J. Wyn (Eds.), *For we are young and... Young people in a time of uncertainty* (pp. 5–28). Melbourne, Australia: Melbourne University Publishing.

Wyn, J., Lantz, S., & Harris, A. (2012). Beyond the 'transitions' metaphor: Family relations and young people in late modernity. *Journal of Sociology, 48*(1), 1–20.

Wyn, J., Smith, G., Stokes, J., Tyler, D., & Woodman, D. (2008). *Generations and social change: Negotiating adulthood in the 21st century.* Melbourne, Australia: Australian Youth Research Centre.

JOHANNA WYN *is a professor in education and director of the Youth Research Centre in the Melbourne Graduate School of Education at The University of Melbourne.*

2

*This chapter discusses the influence of cultural identity and social condi-
tions on the transition to adulthood in a stratified, multicultural context.*

Culture, Conditions, and the Transition to Adulthood

Brendaly Drayton

Demographic, educational, and social implications underlie the importance of
researching and understanding the relationship between cultural identity and
the transition to adulthood. Between 1976 and 2004, minorities at degree-
granting institutions in the United States increased from 17% (1,535,000)
to 32% (4,696,000) of total undergraduate enrollment (KewalRamani,
Gilbertson, Fox, & Provasnik, 2007). Although the five racial groups[1] as outlined by the U.S. Census increased between 2000 and 2010, about half of
the increase was due to the Hispanic population (Humes, Jones, & Ramirez,
2011). In addition, between 2000 and 2009 more than 10 million people became permanent residents in the United States (U.S. Department of Homeland
Security, 2012). The categorization of racial groupings camouflages numerous
ethnic cultures that compose the demographic portrait of the United States.

Research on young adults in adult education has focused primarily on characteristics, motivations, and barriers for continuing education
(Darkenwald & Knox, 1984), and the application of adult development
theory to increase effectiveness of programmatic approaches (Darkenwald,
1984). In terms of youth and culture, Guy (2004), for example, discussed the influence of African American Black popular culture on Black
and White youths in adult education, raising concerns that the cultural
gap between educators and learners restricts possibilities of meeting learner
needs. However, the relationship between culture and the constitution of
motivations and barriers in the transition to adulthood has not been ex-
tensively explored. Culture influences our worldviews, how we interpret
our experiences, how we interact with others, and, to some extent, the
choices we make. Consequently, culture affects student expectations of and
engagement with education as well as educational content and delivery.
Therefore, the diversification of the U.S. population requires educational
approaches that take these factors into consideration. The emergence and
proliferation of multicultural education approaches during the last 50 years

NEW DIRECTIONS FOR ADULT AND CONTINUING EDUCATION, no. 143, Fall 2014 © 2014 Wiley Periodicals, Inc.
Published online in Wiley Online Library (wileyonlinelibrary.com) • DOI: 10.1002/ace.20101

attest to not only the varied needs of students but also the disparities in educational access and outcomes that negatively affect racial, ethnic, and linguistic minorities (Banks, 2006). As such, it is a social justice imperative for adult education to address these concerns (Ross-Gordon, 1990).

This chapter explores how cultural identity and social conditions mediate the transition to adulthood. I approach this topic from a critical sociocultural perspective, which proposes that what constitutes education, how it is valued, and the systems through which it is acquired are culturally shaped and mediated by power relations. As Lewis and Moje (2003) pointed out, adding the critical component expands the purview of sociocultural theory to connect issues of power, agency, and identity to macrostructures of power thereby exposing the sometimes conflicting relationships between society, culture, institutions, and individuals evidenced in daily lived experiences. This chapter provides a background for understanding the role of culture in various educational settings. It begins with an overview of culture and cultural identity followed by a discussion of how culture orients developmental tasks and learning. The second half of the chapter will explore the effects of contact between dominant and minority cultures, concluding with implications for adult education.

Culture and Cultural Identity

Culture is a highly contested concept with numerous definitions spanning many disciplines and philosophical positions. More than 60 years ago, Kroeber and Kluckhohn (1952) listed 164 definitions. In general, culture includes historically based values, beliefs, practices, symbols, meaning systems, languages, and artifacts. The collective nature of culture inheres internal diversity, conflict, and change due to technological, social, and geographical forces (Swidler, 1986). Recognizing that there is no definition that captures culture in its entirety, I draw upon Swidler's concept of culture as a "toolkit" for constructing "strategies of actions" because it focuses on the link between culture and action (p. 277). According to Swidler,

> the symbolic experiences, mythic lore, and ritual practices of a group or society creates moods and motivations, ways of organizing experience and evaluating reality, modes of regulating conduct, and ways of forming social bonds, which provide resources for constructing strategies of action. (p. 284)

In times of social change, entrenched meaning systems provide a basis for new strategies of action in the midst of competing cultural models. However, these resources, and therefore strategies of action, are subject to structural opportunities that influence the pathway to adulthood. Swidler's concept eschews a deterministic view of culture while acknowledging its socializing or orienting power in the construction of individual identity.

New Directions for Adult and Continuing Education • DOI: 10.1002/ace

Identity consists of personal identity characteristics and identification with a social group (Gee, 2000–2001). According to social identity theory (Tajfel & Turner, 1986), cultural or ethnic identity is a subset of social identity, which is identification with a particular group through internalization of values and adoption of practices and beliefs that are mediated by the degree of salience or priority given to the group. In multicultural settings where the subculture is different from the dominant culture, identities become more complex as individuals make decisions about attachments to these groups. In other words, cultural or ethnic identity is distinguished by membership in one's heritage or cultural group and the larger society in which one resides, participation in their practices, and the priority (consciously and unconsciously) given to these groups on a daily basis (Schwartz, Zamboanga, & Weisskirch, 2008). Membership in and level of commitment to the group can hinder or support personal choices and pathways to adulthood. As children develop through adolescence, dimensions of personal identity such as individual values, goals, and beliefs associated with religion, political preference, family and friends' relationship styles, gender role ideologies, and occupational choice (Newman & Newman, 2009) are influenced by their cultural group worldviews.

Culture, Conditions, and the Pathway to Adulthood

Although there are many human development theories, they tend to configure around conceptions of development, factors of cause and effect, and how the elements of satisfactory development are influenced by changing times (Thomas, 1999). Development through the life course involves cognitive, biological, and social dimensions that position individuals within society as they resolve stage or age-based problems (Newman & Newman, 2009). The cultural context shapes the knowledge and value systems supporting these dimensions. Some societies promote an individualistic worldview while others support a communal framework. For example, in the United States and other Western industrialized countries, the transition to adulthood privileges independence and the individual, whereas development in collectivistic-oriented societies elevates interdependence and development of the individual within community (Badger, Nelson, & Barry, 2006; Thomas, 1999). The apparent binary is not meant to obfuscate the presence of individualism in collectivistic societies and vice versa but rather to indicate overarching cultural emphases.

The transition to adulthood can be a process or an event, but it is underpinned by a culture of individualization in Western industrialized societies. In Erikson's (1968) psychosocial model of development, stage transitions hinge on the successful resolution of crises involved in the merging of personal needs with societal expectations. Thus, the transition from the adolescent stage (18–24) to early adulthood (24–34) involves establishing an identity that can effectively adapt to changes in society and relationships throughout the life course (Schwartz, Côté, & Arnett, 2005). Drawing upon Erikson's work, ethnic identity models offer development processes ranging from lack of awareness of ethnic identity through exploration (encountering other groups) to an achieved identity within a multicultural framework (Cross, 1991; Torres, 2003). Psychosocial crises arise through encounters with other cultural or ethnic groups. Ethnic identity theorists note the importance of developing a viable ethnic identity for psychosocial well-being, especially in a multicultural context where particular ethnic groups are disparaged and devalued (Phinney, 1996; Worrell, 2008). It is during this period of trying to find one's place in society that ethnic individuals are sensitized to how they are viewed and treated by the larger society and must make conscious decisions about who they choose to be in light of options available to them.

As a point of comparison between individualistic- and collectivistic-oriented cultures, I draw upon Beckloffs (2008) comparative analysis of Western and traditional African models of human development, where the latter focuses on the development of community (relatedness) and the individual as an integral part of community (interdependency). Since the community sets clear paths for the transition to adulthood and integration into the social structure of society, there is little evidence of a central tendency toward identity and role confusion or issues of isolation versus integration categorized in Erikson's crisis model (Beckloff, 2008, p. 20). The changing economic and social fiber of modern industrialized societies provides weak social and institutional support for the transition to adulthood, hence the prolonged goal of identity exploration and self-actualization (Shanahan, 2000). This is accompanied by the overarching task of acquiring knowledge, skills, and adaptable identities to successfully embrace future opportunities (Schwartz et al., 2005). The indicators and meanings behind the successful completion of developmental tasks are established and sanctioned by society, and therefore are identity markers with implications for societal expectations, rewards for success, and reproach for failure (Havighurst, 1972). The linear progression of life stage models assumes that successful achievement of each stage will lead to well-adjusted productive adults who contribute to the well-being and survival of their societies.

Many studies have shown that age-focused development theories alone are inadequate in explaining the transition to adulthood (Bynner, 2005; Thompson, 2011). Lifespan models contribute to the understanding that the social context is important in shaping human development and in unveiling cultural differences within a given society over time (Thomas, 1999). For example, the sociohistorical life-course theory (Elder, 1998) takes into consideration how societal stability and change, time, and place, as well as the biological and psychological stages of the individual, combine to affect development. Societal factors considered include, but are not limited to, politics, public order and safety, economics, social-class structure, ethnic composition, health conditions, and occupational structure. In sum, lifespan theories envision pathways to adulthood that progress in a given direction based upon previous situations and choices as opposed to progressing through stages. So while culture may dictate particular values, behaviors, and achievements, social factors can promote or constrain access to valorized paths.

Arnett's (2011) cultural theory of emerging adulthood combines both life stage and lifespan theories in the sense that recent changes (e.g., changing views of women's roles, technological advancements, the availability of and increasing need for postsecondary education and training, and a delay in marriage and parenting) in industrialized societies have fostered different perceptions of adulthood and extended the period of transition. Individuals between the ages of 18–25 do not claim adulthood status, but declare that they are in the process of becoming adults with the tasks of achieving independence from parents, taking responsibility for their actions, and exploring committed relationships and career options. This is a move away from the traditional external markers of marriage, employment, parenthood, and high school completion. Arnett (2000) noted that the term "emerging" was more a reflection of the "dynamic, changeable, fluid quality of the period" in their lives and less a reflection of age group (p. 477) and that certain cultural-demographic conditions must exist to support changing perceptions of and pathways to adulthood (Arnett, 2011).

Accordingly, researchers point out that while the emerging adulthood theory has been effective in exposing how our changing society has influenced the transition to adulthood, it has inadequately addressed the varied life paths a stratified and multicultural society such as the United States produces (Côté & Bynner, 2008). For example, studies in the United States, Canada, England, and other European countries (Bynner, 2005) have shown that emerging adulthood is a category that primarily reflects those with the economic resources to allow for prolonged postsecondary education and that the traditional markers of adulthood were more common among socially and economically disadvantaged groups. The primary task of becoming self-sufficient is intimately tied to economic viability; upward mobility factors into discussions and decisions about the pathway to adulthood (Hardaway & McLoyd, 2009).

In the United States, economic constraints often encourage a direct route to work or military service but do not necessarily derail postsecondary aspirations. Due to varying combinations of racism, poverty, and choice, incarceration is a condition of the pathway to adulthood for many economically disadvantaged Hispanic and African American men between the ages of 18–39 (Petitt & Western, 2004; Rios, 2006; Rumbaut, 2005). Postincarceration effects include restriction of available job options, exclusion from federal housing, and significantly restricted funding for education (Oliver, 2010; Pager, 2008). This drastically reduces their ability to meet conventional adulthood markers of independence and self-sufficiency (Raphael, 2007). Research is needed to explore the influence of culture versus social conditions on pathways to adulthood for disadvantaged groups. Environmental conditions and life events are often subsumed under the canopy of culture, leading to deficit identity construction and a disregard for structural factors that shape opportunities and mediate chosen pathways.

Acculturation

Members of ethnic groups must negotiate the expectations of their heritage group and those of the dominant cultural group that underpins the social institutions of society. Consequently, acculturation (the degree to which the individual orients toward the dominant culture) must be considered when exploring cultural influences on the transition to adulthood. Ethnic identity is a nonissue in a monocultural society; prolonged contact with other cultures affects how members see themselves in relation to others and experience the ensuing lived realities of that interaction (Phinney, 1996). Individuals whose cultures are different from the dominant culture encounter more dissonance than those whose cultures are similar (Thomas, 1999). This is compounded for ethnic groups of color that confront unequal access to power and resources, pervasive negative stereotyping, and discrimination in the midst of a dominant White majority (Hardaway & McLoyd, 2009; Phinney, 1996). Certainly, the degree to which this dissonance is experienced on an individual basis is contingent upon a variety of factors such as class, ethnic group, sociopolitical structure of the region, and the organizations of which the individual is a member.

Berry, Trimble, and Olmedo (1986) offered four possible responses to cross-cultural contact depending on strength of identification with either group: (a) strong identification with both groups suggests integration or biculturalism, (b) weak identification with both indicates minimal identification with either, (c) strong identification with the dominant group and minimal identification with the heritage group points to assimilation, and (d) strong identification with the heritage group and minimal with the dominant group suggests separation. Ethnic identity scholarship indicates that ethnic identity holds greater salience for minority groups in general than for the dominant group (Hardaway & McLoyd, 2009; Phinney, 1996) whose culture tends to be intertwined with social structure and accepted as the norm (Chavez & Guido-DiBrito, 1999; Swidler, 1986). This may be due in part to the significance of ethnic group identity in shaping their social and economic lives.

In fact, Jackson (1999) found that negotiation of cultural identity, the "process in which one considers the gain, loss, or exchange of their ability to interpret their own reality or worldview," was a marginalized group phenomenon (p. 10). In other words, it is a circumstance of inequitable power relations. The "negotiation of cultural identity" is played out in daily interactions in concrete settings where policies and practices of social institutions often align with the dominant culture and constitute particular expectations and identities. The degree to which an individual's "cultural toolkit" aligns with organizational culture mediates the ease with which progress is achieved (Hardaway & McLoyd, 2009). Members from different cultural groups

New Directions for Adult and Continuing Education • DOI: 10.1002/ace

experience culture shock. It is the awareness of difference during prolonged periods of cross-cultural contact and the psychological, emotional, and physical distress that comes from the sense of isolation and alienation (Furnham & Bochner, 1986). Also, it is the recognition that ways of being and doing are questioned, not effective, and not valued in the new environment.

Swidler (1986) noted that "cultural expertise" supports the abilities of the individual to construct effective strategies of action (p. 281). Consequently, the individual must consider "cultural retooling" in terms of communicative practices and skills that are needed to be successful in a new environment (p. 277). An organization's sensitivity and receptiveness to diverse cultural orientations and the individual's strength of attachment to cultural heritage mediate the process. Some individuals may see cultural retooling as pressure to assimilate and choose to support their cultural identity by separating themselves from the organization or enhancing their cultural identity by cleaving to members of their cultural group. Others may consider "cultural retooling" as learning the "culture of power" (Delpit, 1988), taking advantage of available opportunities in the larger society to pursue upward mobility and economic independence. The latter does not imply a sacrifice of cultural identity but rather drawing strength from the heritage culture to participate in other cultural worlds (Chavez & Guido-DiBrito, 1999). So the transition to adulthood for members of minority ethnic groups includes not only developing a viable identity that will adapt to future changes, establishing independence, exploring career options and relationship commitments, but also preserving their cultural identity while learning to walk in two worlds. Associated skill sets may include mode switching and code switching, learning behavior and language patterns that would allow them to function effectively in different social contexts (Baynham, 1993; White & Lowenthal, 2011).

Biculturalism is common among emerging adults, especially as it relates to collectivism and individualism. Many of the ethnic cultures in the United States align with a collectivistic orientation. In a study on the perceptions of adulthood, Hispanic Americans, African Americans, and Asian Americans tended to demonstrate biculturalism by adopting the individualism of the dominant culture while maintaining a high salience for family obligations and community values (Arnett, 2003). Independence consistently appeared as a primary factor in the criteria for achieving adulthood status but with different cultural meanings. For instance, financial independence for Chinese Americans had the underlying purpose of providing financial support for parents as opposed to simply being self-sufficient (Badger et al., 2006). Also among high-traditional Canadian aboriginal college students, independence, as in making decisions and being accountable for one's choices, would not be considered a developmental task but rather maintaining a cultural value (Cheah & Nelson, 2004). Children from many indigenous cultures in North America are taught from very young to be independent because they believe that no one should speak for another or control their actions (Cheah & Nelson, 2004, p. 496). These studies reflect the large pool of research on college students; they also highlight the need for research on others who choose alternate pathways. It is possible that the college environment may skew results toward a general trend of biculturalism. This raises the question: How significant is the developmental task of learning to walk in two worlds for other settings and different socioeconomic groups?

Implications for Adult Education

The transition to adulthood involves the acquisition of skills and abilities that afford achievement of particular goals deemed necessary for adulthood status, and more importantly, for individual and collective well-being. Adult education can play a critical role in the process by constructing learning opportunities that support emerging adult developmental tasks and meet the needs of ethnically and culturally diverse populations. Globalization and the changing nature of our society stress the importance of cultural competence for educators and learners.

Cultural competence is a combination of knowledge, attitudes, and skills used to promote equal access and opportunities (Banks, 2006; Sue, 2001). Adult educators can help learners achieve their goals by employing strategies that would reduce alienation and isolation for the learner. Educational environments insensitive to cultural and ethnic differences impede success and promote attrition (Kirkness & Barnhardt, 1991). Cultural competence calls for an intentional critique of social structures, organizational practices and policies, and learner–educator relationships to expose taken-for-granted assumptions that foster inequity, exclusion, and oppression. Some of the questions teachers can ask include: How much do I know about the lived experiences of the groups represented in the classroom? What subliminal messages am I sending about different groups through the omission and selection of texts? What knowledge (e.g., widely accepted ideas about a particular group and personal experiences) am I drawing upon to interpret behaviors, determine what is good, and inform my interaction with others?

As emerging adults prepare for roles in the workplace, community, and other social environments, adult educators can enhance learners' abilities to interact with people from diverse cultures in a variety of organizational settings. Educators can use texts from different cultures, collaborative projects, and dialogue as standard practice in the classroom to help learners examine their own individual cultural leanings and prejudices, learn about different cultures, and unearth miscommunications and misinterpretations that can arise in such settings. Banks (2006) cautioned that the selection of particular days or units to focus on minority and ethnic groups reinforced the idea of such groups as being separate from U.S. society. Brookfield's (2012) *Teaching for Critical Thinking: Tools and Techniques to Help Students Question Their Assumptions* is an excellent resource, especially for engaging students who might be resistant to ideas that challenge their worldviews. In addition, as emerging adults seek to establish psychological independence from parents, critical thinking enhances their skill and confidence in making informed decisions. There are many strategies of action within a "cultural toolkit" but the choice and success of an appropriated strategy depend on the availability of capacities to support it.

Note

1. The five race categories used in the 2010 U.S. Census are: White, Black or African American, American Indian or Alaska Native, Asian, and Native Hawaiian or other Pacific Islander. There is also a category for Other race. Those of mixed heritage may self-identify as Other race. Hispanic origin is considered an ethnicity. Consequently those who identify as Hispanic, Spanish, or Latino must choose from among the racial categories.

References

Arnett, J. J. (2000). Emerging adulthood. *American Psychologist, 55*(5), 469–480.

Arnett, J. J. (2003). Conceptions of the transition to adulthood among emerging adults in American ethnic groups. In J. J. Arnett & N. L. Galambos (Eds.), *New Directions for Child and Adolescent Development: No. 100. Exploring cultural conceptions of the transition to adulthood* (pp. 63–76). San Francisco, CA: Jossey-Bass.

Arnett, J. J. (2011). Emerging adulthoods: The cultural psychology of a new stage. In L. Jenson (Ed.), *Bridging cultural and developmental approaches to psychology* (pp. 255–275). New York, NY: Oxford University Press.

Badger, S., Nelson, L., & Barry, C. (2006). Perceptions of the transition to adulthood among Chinese and American emerging adults. *International Journal of Behavioral Development, 30*(1), 84–93.

Banks, J. (2006). *Cultural diversity and education: Foundations, curriculum, and teaching* (5th ed.). New York, NY: Pearson.

Baynham, M. (1993). Code switching and mode switching: Community interpreters and mediators of literacy. In B. Street (Ed.), *Cross-cultural approaches to literacy* (pp. 294–314). Cambridge, UK: Cambridge University Press.

Beckloff, R. (2008). Cross-cultural perspectives on adult development: Implications for adult education in Africa. *Convergence, 41*(2–3), 13–26.

Berry, J., Trimble, J., & Olmedo, J. (1986). Assessment of acculturation. In W. Lonner & J. Berry (Eds.), *Field methods in cross-cultural research* (pp. 291–324). Newberry Park, CA: Sage.

Brookfield, S. (2012). *Teaching for critical thinking: Tools and techniques to help students question their assumptions*. San Francisco, CA: Jossey-Bass.

Bynner, J. (2005). Rethinking the youth phase of the life course: The case of emerging adulthood? *Journal of Youth Studies, 8*(4), 367–384.

Chavez, A., & Guido-DiBrito, F. (1999). Racial and ethnic identity development. In M. C. Clark & R. S. Caffarella (Eds.), *New Directions for Adult and Continuing Education: No. 84. An update on adult development theory: New ways of thinking about the life course* (pp. 39–46). San Francisco, CA: Jossey-Bass.

Cheah, C., & Nelson, L. (2004). The role of acculturation in the emerging adulthood of aboriginal college students. *International Journal of Behavioral Development, 28*(6), 495–507.

Côté, J., & Bynner, J. (2008). Changes in the transition to adulthood in the U.K. and Canada: The role of structure and agency in emerging adulthood. *Journal of Youth Studies, 11*(3), 251–268.

Cross, W. (1991). *Shades of black: Diversity in African American identity*. Philadelphia, PA: Temple University.

Darkenwald, G. (1984). Participation in education by young adults. In G. Darkenwald & A. Knox (Eds.), *New Directions for Continuing Education: No. 21. Meeting the educational needs of young adults* (pp. 99–105). San Francisco, CA: Jossey-Bass.

Darkenwald, G., & Knox, A. (1984). Themes and issues in programming for young adults. In G. Darkenwald & A. Knox (Eds.), *New Directions for Continuing Education: No. 21. Meeting the educational needs of young adults* (pp. 15–28). San Francisco, CA: Jossey-Bass.

Delpit, L. (1988). The silenced dialogue: Power and pedagogy in educating other people's children. *Harvard Educational Review, 58*(3), 280–298.

Elder, G. (1998). The life course as developmental theory. *Child Development, 69*(1), 1–12.

Erikson, E. H. (1968). *Identity: Youth and crisis.* Oxford, UK: Norton.

Furnham, A., & Bochner, S. (1986). *Culture shock: Psychological reactions to unfamiliar environments.* London, UK: Methuen.

Gee, J. (2000–2001). Identity as an analytic lens for research in education. *Review of Research in Education, 25,* 99–125.

Guy, T. (2004). Gangsta rap and adult education. In L. Martin & E. Rogers (Eds.), *New Directions for Continuing Education: No. 101. Adult education in an urban context* (pp. 43–58). San Francisco, CA: Jossey-Bass.

Hardaway, C., & McLoyd, V. C. (2009). Escaping poverty and securing middle-class status: How race and socioeconomic status shape mobility prospects for African Americans during the transition to adulthood. *Journal of Youth and Adolescence, 38,* 242–256.

Havighurst, R. (1972). *Developmental tasks and education.* New York, NY: David McKay.

Humes, K., Jones, N., & Ramirez, R. (2011). Overview of race and Hispanic origin: 2010. *2010 Census Briefs.* Washington, DC: U.S. Census Bureau.

Jackson, R., II. (1999). *The negotiation of cultural identity: Perceptions of Europeans and African Americans.* Westport, CT: Praeger.

KewalRamani, A., Gilbertson, L., Fox, M., & Provasnik, S. (2007). *Status and trends in the education of racial and ethnic minorities* (NCES 2007–039). Washington, DC: U.S. Department of Education.

Kirkness, V., & Barnhardt, R. (1991). First nations and higher education: The four Rs— respect, relevance, reciprocity, and responsibility. *Journal of American Indian Education, 30*(3), 1–15.

Kroeber, A., & Kluckhohn, C. (1952). *Culture: A critical review of concepts and definitions.* Papers of the Peabody Museum of Archaeology & Ethnology (Vol. 47, No. 1). Cambridge, MA: Harvard University.

Lewis, C., & Moje, E. (2003). Sociocultural perspectives meet critical theories. *International Journal of Learning, 10,* 1979–1995.

Newman, B., & Newman, P. (2009). *Development through life: A psychosocial approach* (10th ed.). Belmont, CA: Wadsworth Cengage Learning.

Oliver, B. (2010). My sentence is over but will my punishment ever end. *Dialectical Anthropology, 34*(4), 447–451.

Pager, D. (2008). Blacklisted: Hiring discrimination in an era of mass incarceration. In E. Anderson (Ed.), *Against the wall: Poor, young, black, and male* (pp. 71–86). Philadelphia: University of Pennsylvania Press.

Petitt, B., & Western, B. (2004). Mass imprisonment and the lifecourse: Race and class inequality in US incarceration. *American Sociological Review, 69*(2), 151–169.

Phinney, J. (1996). Understanding ethnic diversity: The role of ethnic identity. *American Behavioral Scientist, 40*(2), 143–152.

Raphael, S. (2007). Early incarceration spells and the transition to adulthood. In S. Danzinger & C. E. Rouse (Eds.), *The price of independence: The economics of early adulthood* (pp. 278–306). New York, NY: Russell Sage Foundation.

Rios, V. (2006). The hyper-criminalization of Black and Latino male youth in the era of mass incarceration. *Souls: A Critical Journal of Black Politics, Culture, and Society, 8*(2), 40–54.

Ross-Gordon, J. (1990). Serving culturally diverse populations: A social imperative for adult and continuing education. In J. M. Ross-Gordon, L. G. Martin, & D. B. Briscoe (Eds.), *New Directions for Adult and Continuing Education: No. 48. Serving culturally diverse populations* (pp. 5–15). San Francisco, CA: Jossey-Bass.

Rumbaut, R. (2005). Turning points in the transition to adulthood: Determinants of educational attainment, incarceration, and early childbearing among children of immigrants. *Ethnic and Racial Studies, 28*(6), 1041–1086.

Schwartz, S., Côté, J., & Arnett, J. (2005). Identity and agency in emerging adulthood: Two developmental routes in the individualization process. *Youth & Society, 37*(2), 201–229.

Schwartz, S., Zamboanga, B., & Weisskirch, B. (2008). Broadening the study of the self: Integrating the study of personal identity and cultural identity. *Social and Psychology Personality Compass, 2*(2), 635–651.

Shanahan, M. (2000). Pathways to adulthood in changing societies: Variability and mechanisms in life course perspective. *Annual Review of Sociology, 26*, 667–692.

Sue, D. (2001). Multidimensional facets of cultural competence. *The Counseling Psychologist, 29*(6), 790–822.

Swidler, A. (1986). Culture in action: Symbols and strategies. *American Sociological Review, 51*(2), 273–286.

Tajfel, H., & Turner, J. (1986). The social identity theory of inter-group behaviors. In S. Worchel & L. W. Austin (Eds.), *Social identity and inter-group relations* (pp. 7–24). Chicago, IL: Nelson-Hall.

Thomas, R. (1999). *Human development theories: Windows on culture*. Thousand Oaks, CA: Sage.

Thompson, R. (2011). Individualisation and social exclusion: The case of young people not in education, employment or training. *Oxford Review of Education, 37*(6), 785–802.

Torres, V. (2003). Influences on ethnic identity development of Latino college students in the first two years of college. *Journal of College Student Development, 44*(4), 532–547.

U.S. Department of Homeland Security. (2012). *Yearbook of immigration statistics: 2011.* Washington, DC: Office of Immigration Statistics.

White, J., & Lowenthal, P. (2011). Minority college students and tacit "codes of power": Developing academic discourses and identities. *Review of Higher Education, 34*(2), 283–318.

Worrell, F. (2008). Nigrescence attitudes in adolescence, emerging adulthood, and adulthood. *Journal of Black Psychology, 34*(2), 156–178.

BRENDALY DRAYTON *is a graduate of the doctoral program in adult education at Pennsylvania State University.*

3

This chapter focuses on vulnerable youth, the challenges they face during their transitions to adulthood, and the adverse effects of limited support systems on those transitions. The authors offer recommendations on how adult educators can help facilitate smooth transitions into adulthood for vulnerable youth.

Vulnerable Youth and Transitions to Adulthood

Rongbing Xie, Bisakha (Pia) Sen, E. Michael Foster

Transitions into adulthood are critical phases in which adolescents and young adults experience change and learn to be physically, psychologically, financially, and socially competent for adult responsibilities. A smooth transition into adulthood can serve as a good start toward a happy and successful adulthood. To complete the transition, one has to fulfill educational goals, become economically self-sufficient, and develop and maintain affirming social relationships. Attaining these goals is increasingly complex in contemporary society, and it is even more complex and often takes longer to accomplish for youth who are considered vulnerable.

We define *vulnerable youth* as "those that often suffer from emotional and behavioral problems and have a history of problems in the school and community" (Osgood, Foster, Flanagan, & Ruth, 2005, p. 2). Among all the young people pursuing independence, vulnerable youth are expected to suffer the greatest burden and have the worst outcomes, since they are likely to be facing disadvantages ranging from low socioeconomic status, lack of family support, subpar foster care, mental health issues, failure to complete school, teen parenthood, or crime records. These youth struggle to enter adult roles, and they often require services from public systems such as mental health care, welfare, or juvenile/adult justice systems. Lacking developmentally appropriate support for transitions to adulthood, these youth may stay in poverty and deprivation, giving birth to children who are then also raised in poverty, and resulting in great cost to society with regard to resources and efforts.

Dr. Foster passed away on May 15, 2013, after a long battle with cancer. This chapter is dedicated to him and his exceptional contribution to this research field.

NEW DIRECTIONS FOR ADULT AND CONTINUING EDUCATION, no. 143, Fall 2014 © 2014 Wiley Periodicals, Inc.
Published online in Wiley Online Library (wileyonlinelibrary.com) • DOI: 10.1002/ace.20102

Vulnerable youth may often find themselves "aging out" of available support systems designed to care for children and youth before they have truly transitioned into adulthood. Therefore, adult education is essential to preparing them for higher education and careers, and effective adult education programs tailored to meet their complex needs can be of immense help. More importantly, adult educators can motivate and lead these youth to learn, find meaning in life, and provide themselves hope for a better future. This chapter presents information that may be useful to adult educators in terms of who vulnerable youth are and what challenges they face. The chapter ends by suggesting some strategies that adult educators can adopt to enhance outcomes for this population.

Background of Vulnerable Youth and Their Transitions to Adulthood

Vulnerable youth are individuals aged 16–24, who have difficulties achieving educational goals, becoming and staying gainfully employed, and obtaining social support needed for a successful transition to adulthood (TAYSF, 2007). Up to 10% of youth between 16 and 24—approximately four million youth nationwide—are vulnerable (Howden & Meyer, 2010). Vulnerable youth are more likely to be racial and ethnic minorities, come from low-income and unstable families, and have a higher risk of having poor academic performance and low employability; they may remain physically and mentally distressed, abusing substances, and engaging in criminal activities (Osgood, Foster, & Courtney, 2010). Among vulnerable populations, youth who have been involved with mental health residential care, foster care, or juvenile/adult justice systems experience the most challenging transitions and are at the greatest risk for yielding poor transitional outcomes. Understanding who these youth are can prepare adult educators for tailoring interventions to address their distinctive needs.

Youth in the Mental Health Care System. Approximately 50,000 youths are admitted to mental health residential care each year, after having been diagnosed with severe mental health conditions, alcohol and other drug abuse, or mood and disruptive behavior disorders (Dinges et al., 2008). During their transitions into adulthood, youth are transferred from pediatric to adult mental health care systems, and they face forced interruptions in continuity of care and disconnections of desirable services (Crowley, Wolfe, Lock, & McKee, 2011; Singh, 2009). The resulting changes in environment, culture, and treatment plans can affect these youth's cognitive and social development (Costello, Copeland, & Angold, 2011). Additionally, more than 50% of students with emotional disturbances drop out of school, which is substantially higher than drop-out rates for youth with any disability (28.9%; Wagner, 1995). Wagner and Newman (2012) followed youth with emotional disturbances for four years during transitions into adulthood. In the end, 82.5% of these young adults had completed high school, half had obtained some postsecondary education, and half were unemployed. More than 60% had lived without adult support and supervision, 60% had been arrested at least once, and about half had been on probation or parole.

Foster Youth Who Age Out of the Child Welfare System. More than 400,000 children and adolescents live in foster care, and each year about 20,000 youth age out of the system (Courtney & Heuring, 2005). Foster children may have a history of maltreatment including neglect (60%), physical abuse (20%), or sexual abuse (10%; Census, 2012). Maltreatment experiences increase the lifetime likelihood of developing at least one psychiatric disorder to three times the rates of the general youth population: 61% for those who have experienced maltreatment versus 20% in the general youth population (McMillen et al., 2005).

During transitions to adulthood, foster care alumni have a high school completion rate comparable to their mainstream peers, but a high number of them obtain a GED rather than a high school diploma; furthermore, they have low postsecondary education completion rates (Courtney et al., 2011). One third of former foster children do not have health insurance, one third live at or below the poverty line, and one fifth experience homelessness after aging out of foster care. Courtney et al. found two factors—a stable placement history and having been prepared for independent living with concrete resources when leaving care—were correlated with better educational outcomes for former foster care youth.

Juvenile and Young Adult Offenders Who Reenter the Community. In 2009, more than 6.5 million juveniles aged 16–17 were under juvenile court jurisdiction, and more than 20,000 youth younger than 25 were sentenced as adult prisoners in 2011 (Carson & Sabol, 2012; Puzzanchera, Adams, & Hockenberry, 2012). Being incarcerated and holding criminal records can limit one's capabilities and connections to reach educational and career goals (Chung, Little, & Steinberg, 2005). Bullis, Yovanoff, Mueller, and Havel (2002) found only 30% of young ex-offenders were involved in school or work a year after they had reentered the community. In contrast, since criminal "social capital" and "human capital" are relatively easy to obtain for these youth, it becomes more convenient for a young ex-offender to pursue a criminal career when securing a legitimate job is difficult (Nguyen & Bouchard, 2013).

Multi-System Youth. Finally, youth who have been involved in more than one system are referred to as "multi-system youth" (Herz et al., 2012). These youth can be foster children in and out of correctional facilities, juvenile offenders with mental disabilities, or foster children with mental disorders or substance abuse issues (Geary, 2013; Herz et al., 2012). Overlaps in combinations of systems are extensive, and these multi-system youth stand out from their vulnerable peers as the ones with the worst experiences and the poorest outcomes (Chuang & Wells, 2010; Osgood et al., 2010).

In summary, vulnerable populations share similar characteristics, histories, and issues. At the same time, these individuals present diverse needs and complex outcomes. Early interventions and trainings are essential to improving these disadvantaged youth's transitions into adults.

What Challenges Are Vulnerable Youth Facing?

To successfully transition to adulthood, vulnerable youth often navigate a complicated path. Difficulties may include regaining mental health stability, reducing substance dependence, establishing functional and trustful intimate relationships despite having been maltreated, building competencies and connections in a relatively restrictive environment, acquiring independent housing with limited or no family support, and overcoming social stigma and discrimination. These extra challenges may leave less time and fewer resources for vulnerable youth to pursue academic achievement and enhance employability (Altschuler, 2005).

Inadequate Competencies. Although vulnerable youth face additional challenges, these youth often do not have adequate competencies to cope. Youth with mental disorders are often less able to control their emotions and behaviors, and some of them have learning difficulties; subsequently, these youth lack the competencies to meet academic requirements, work requests, or social needs (Gralinski-Bakker, Hauser, Billings, & Allen, 2005). Similarly, foster care alumni are at a higher risk (30%) of presenting symptoms of posttraumatic stress disorders (PTSD) such as depression, anxiety, and aggression than their community peers (7.6%); accordingly, these symptoms impair cognitive development and psychosocial functioning (Courtney, Hook, & Lee, 2012). Moreover, about two thirds of youth involved with justice systems have mental health disorders, and these disorders combined with criminal records decrease their chances of obtaining education, training, and employment (Nguyen & Bouchard, 2013).

Insufficient Social Support. Compared to mainstream youth, vulnerable youth have far less social support for transitions to adulthood. First, these youth may lack a stable family, caring parents, and may have been unwanted in the first place. Moreover, their parents (or parental figures) may have ongoing violence, substance abuse, mental disorders, and educational and employment challenges as well as criminal activities themselves, which may bring on and subsequently worsen emotional and behavior problems for these youth (Murray, Farrington, & Sekol, 2012). Therefore, these families do not have the capacity to provide vulnerable youth with suitable role models or with sufficient emotional, financial, and educational support.

Second, vulnerable youth may not have psychologically available adults to help them develop autonomy, self-governance, and social competencies (Allen & Hauser, 1996). Parents with mentally ill children commonly feel stressed, guilty, sad, or exhausted; equally, children who have been discharged from residential care have a hard time bonding with their distressed parents and are more likely to run away (Embry, Vander Stoep, Evens, Ryan, & Pollock, 2000). Similarly, foster care alumni have received little economic or emotional support for education from their guardians; meanwhile, lacking placement and educational stability makes becoming attached to teachers extremely difficult (Sullivan, Jones, & Mathiesen, 2010). The situation is at least as bleak in the juvenile/adult justice systems. Staff members frequently use physical punishment and humiliation, but these regulatory methods are actually ineffective and thwart the establishment of positive youth–staff relationships (Bartollas, Miller, & Dinitz, 1976; Marsh, Evans, & Williams, 2010). An absence of supportive adults in transitions reduces vulnerable youth's likelihood of exploring adult roles (Chung et al., 2005).

Finally, social stigma directed at vulnerable youth significantly limits social support from family, school, and community. In one study on stigma experiences among mentally ill youth, nearly half of participants reported discrimination by family members, 62% experienced peer stigmatization, and one third described stigma perpetrated by school staff (Moses, 2010). Moreover, foster youth often withdraw from peer interaction to hide their foster care status (Finkelstein, Wamsley, & Miranda, 2002). Likewise, young people with criminal records bear with stigma and discrimination in both education and employment settings (Finlay, 2012; Sander et al., 2011).

In conclusion, vulnerable youth take a longer time and rougher route to be psychologically competent and financially independent (Osgood et al., 2010). On the one hand, these youth have more barriers and challenges to overcome; on the other hand, they experience not only a lack of competencies, resources, and social support but also stigma and discrimination. These youth are likely from unstable families missing parental support, and therefore heavily dependent on our system support to meet their transitional needs.

Adverse Effects of a Limited Support System. Public systems designed to help vulnerable youth often fail to meet their needs due to system-level service delivery failures. These can result from limited resources or budget cuts, which affect both quality and quantity of services (Chorpita, Bernstein, & Daleiden, 2011). For instance, during the 2011 fiscal year, Colorado eliminated funding for more than 600 patients receiving residential treatment in state-owned mental health institutes (Johnson, Oliff, & Williams, 2011). There is also the problem of fragmented services. Potential consequences of fragmented services include unidentified needs, undertreated individuals, and duplicated efforts (Friedman, Greenbaum, Wang, Kutash, & Boothroyd, 2009). Ideally, public staff should connect youth with unmet needs to other appropriate agencies; for example, social workers identify foster children with severe emotional disturbance and send these children to the mental health care system (Bunger, Stiffman, Foster, & Shi, 2010). In reality, staff members may not be able to perform mental health needs assessment. Even if they can, staff may remain unaware of available services in other agencies (Bunger et al., 2010). Rather than utilizing existing services offered by other agencies, some agencies may try to "reinvent the wheel" by ineffectively and inefficiently providing services not within their realm of expertise (Courtney & Heuring, 2005).

The final problem is that of "aging out" of child-serving systems and losing developmentally proper system support (Courtney et al., 2012). Physically attaining a certain age (such as 18 or 21) does not guarantee transition to adulthood. Yet, foster children aging out of the system can find themselves facing termination of housing, health care, psychosocial and financial support, and educational opportunities (Courtney & Heuring, 2005). Delinquent youth in juvenile facilities may be transferred to adult correctional facilities, where they are at an increased risk of abuse and distress (Levitt, 2010; Ng, Sarri, Shook, & Stoffregen, 2012). Aging out often involves a desperate hunt for life skill trainings and extended medical care, with limited information about how to access or evaluate the quality of services (McConkey, Kelly, Mannan, & Craig, 2010; Neutens, Schwanen, Witlox, & De Maeyer, 2010).

The Contributions of Adult Educators to Successful Transitions

While adult educators may not be familiar with the term "vulnerable youth," they may often find these students in their basic education and GED classrooms. Adult educators may sense frustration over the demanding teaching requirements and low educational outcomes associated with these populations (Jones, Dohrn, & Dunn, 2004). To support success in learning during transitions into adulthood, in addition to providing effective educational programs, adult educators should lead vulnerable youth to build relevant competencies, offer these youth social support, and connect them to needed resources and services.

Build Competencies. Adult educators can individualize teaching materials and activities based on vulnerable youth's current subject-related skills, personal and social capability, and linguistic needs. Furthermore, educational and vocational programs can be individualized and tailored, thanks to technological advances (Walsh, Lemon, Black, Mangan, & Collin, 2011). In addition, evidence-based teaching methods with relevant information are increasingly used to deliver trainings to vulnerable youth in a flexible and satisfying manner (Marsh et al., 2010).

Initially, adult educators nurture vulnerable youth's sustainable learning skills by persistently providing guidance, support, assessment, and feedback. Once these young adults have mastered basic skills and built self-confidence, adult educators can involve learners in challenging tasks. This may serve to engage learners in deeply understanding and strategically applying concepts to solve daily problems and situations (OECD, 2006).

Provide Social Support. Respectful relationships are a solid foundation of teaching, training, and learning (Wlodkowski, 2011). To foster close relationships, educators must promote youth's social and emotional health, offer more opportunities to learn relationship-building skills, and cultivate active learning by creating excitement in teaching (Bonwell & Eison, 1991; van Uden, Ritzen, & Pieters, 2014). More importantly, strong relationships with teachers and peer students can create an effective and supportive learning community, which allows learners to collaborate in groups, learn from each other, and stay inspired to achieve success in learning (OECD, 2006).

Equally, inclusion—that is, a feeling of safety and acceptance—is key to enhancing vulnerable youth's cognitive process of receiving, analyzing, and storing complex information (Wlodkowski, 2011). Inclusion can shield vulnerable youth from discrimination and stigma, and it can encourage the learner's motivation and involvement. Adult educators can integrate inclusion into learning by being sympathetic listeners who understand vulnerable youth's challenges and cheering facilitators who actively enable vulnerable youth to find meaning and hope in their learning and lives.

Make Connections to Resources and Services. Adult educators can support vulnerable youth's success in learning by overcoming system-level barriers and obtaining needed resources and services for these youth to fulfill their roles, accomplish daily tasks, and deal with difficulties in the outside world (OECD, 2006). Specifically, adult educators need to be familiar with an array of local services, from housing assistance, employment services, welfare services, mental health care services, educational and vocational programs to learning disability services (Becerra & Moore, 2009; Hudson, 2006). Bridging the resource and service gap can ease the lives of vulnerable youths and eventually help them achieve educational goals and excellence.

Conclusions

Overall, living as healthy, productive, and independent adults for vulnerable youth is a difficult—but not impossible—challenge. And yet, a just society should provide all youth the opportunity to grow up in a caring and supportive environment, despite constrained resources and fragmented systems. The greater society is responsible for offering these disadvantaged youth what they need for a successful transition to adulthood. Society cannot control the circumstances of birth or the initial familial environment into which vulnerable youth are born, but systems can be improved. More importantly, adult educators can play a vital role in ensuring that vulnerable youth are not left ignored and isolated.

References

Allen, J. P., & Hauser, S. T. (1996). Autonomy and relatedness in adolescent-family interactions as predictors of young adults' states of mind regarding attachment. *Development and Psychopathology, 8*, 793–810.

Altschuler, D. M. (2005). Policy and program perspectives on the transition to adulthood for adolescents in the juvenile justice system. In D. W. Osgood, E. M. Foster, C. Flanagan, & G. R. Ruth (Eds.), *On your own without a net: The transition to adulthood for vulnerable populations* (pp. 92–113). Chicago, IL: The University of Chicago Press.

Bartollas, C., Miller, S. J., & Dinitz, S. (1976). *Juvenile victimization: The institutional paradox.* Thousand Oaks, CA: Sage.

Becerra, C., & Moore, A. (2009). *Supporting foster youth transitions to adulthood.* Washington, DC: Institute for Youth, Education, and Families.

Bonwell, C. C., & Eison, J. A. (1991). *Active learning: Creating excitement in the classroom.* Washington, DC: School of Education and Human Development, George Washington University.

Bullis, M., Yovanoff, P., Mueller, G., & Havel, E. (2002). Life on the "outs"—Examination of the facility-to-community transition of incarcerated youth. *Exceptional Children, 69*(1), 7–22.

Bunger, A. C., Stiffman, A. R., Foster, K. A., & Shi, P. (2010). Child welfare workers' connectivity to resources and youth's receipt of services. *Advances in Social Work, 10*(1), 19–38.

Carson, E. A., & Sabol, W. J. (2012). Prisoners in 2011. *Prisoners series.* Washington DC: Office of Justice Programs. Retrieved from http://www.doc.wa.gov /aboutdoc/measuresstatistics/docs/BJSReport.Prisonersin2011.pdf

Census. (2012). *Table 342. Child abuse and neglect victims by selected characteristics: 2000 to 2009. U.S. Census Bureau, Statistical Abstract of the United States:* 2012. Retrieved from https://www.census.gov/compendia/statab/2012/tables/12s0342.pdf

Chorpita, B. F., Bernstein, A., & Daleiden, E. L. (2011). Empirically guided coordination of multiple evidence-based treatments: An illustration of relevance mapping in children's mental health services. *Journal of Consulting and Clinical Psychology, 79*(4), 470–480.

Chuang, E., & Wells, R. (2010). The role of inter-agency collaboration in facilitating receipt of behavioral health services for youth involved with child welfare and juvenile justice. *Children and Youth Services Review, 32*(12), 1814–1822.

Chung, H. L., Little, M., & Steinberg, L. (2005). *The transition to adulthood for adolescents in the juvenile justice system: A developmental perspective.* Chicago, IL: University of Chicago Press.

Costello, E. J., Copeland, W., & Angold, A. (2011). Trends in psychopathology across the adolescent years: What changes when children become adolescents, and when adolescents become adults? *Journal of Child Psychology and Psychiatry, 52*(10), 1015–1025.

Courtney, M. E., Dworsky, A., Brown, A., Cary, C., Love, K., & Vorhies, V. (2011). *Midwest evaluation of the adult functioning of former foster youth: Outcomes at age 26.* Chicago, IL: Chapin Hall at the University of Chicago. Retrieved from http://www.chapinhall .org/sites/default/files/Midwest%20Evaluation_Report_4_10_12.pdf

Courtney, M. E., & Heuring, D. H. (2005). The transition to adulthood for youth "aging out" of the foster care system. In D. W. Osgood, E. M. Foster, C. Flanagan, & G. R. Ruth (Eds.), *On your own without a net: The transition to adulthood for vulnerable populations* (pp. 27–67). Chicago, IL: The University of Chicago Press.

Courtney, M. E., Hook, J. L., & Lee, J. S. (2012). Distinct subgroups of former foster youth during young adulthood: Implications for policy and practice. *Child Care in Practice, 18*(4), 409–418.

Crowley, R., Wolfe, I., Lock, K., & McKee, M. (2011). Improving the transition between paediatric and adult healthcare: A systematic review. *Archives of Disease in Childhood, 96*(6), 548–553.

Dinges, K., Discher, J., Leopold, M., Matyas, C., Ruiz, C., Marciano, D., . . . Happ, D. (2008). *Perspectives on residential and community-based treatment for youth and families.* Avon, CT: Magellan Health Services Children's Services Task Force. Retrieved from http://www.mtfc.com/2008%20Magellan%20RTC%20White%20Paper.pdf

Embry, L. E., Vander Stoep, A. V., Evens, C., Ryan, K. D., & Pollock, A. (2000). Risk factors for homelessness in adolescents released from psychiatric residential treatment. *Journal of the American Academy of Child & Adolescent Psychiatry, 39*(10), 1293–1299.

Finkelstein, M., Wamsley, M., & Miranda, D. (2002). *What keeps children in foster care from succeeding in school?: Views of early adolescents and the adults in their lives.* New York, NY: Vera Institute of Justice. Retrieved from http://www.vera.org/sites/default/files/resources /downloads/School_success.pdf

Finlay, K. (2012). *Stigma in the labor market: Evidence from juveniles transferred to adult court and occupations with mandated criminal background checks.* Paper presented at the 2013 American Economic Association Conference, San Diego, CA. Retrieved from http://www.aeaweb.org/aea/2013conference/program/retrieve.php?pdfid=367

Friedman, R. M., Greenbaum, P. E., Wang, W., Kutash, K., & Boothroyd, R. (2009). System of care implementation. *Mental Health Law & Policy Faculty Publications.* Paper 492. Retrieved from http://scholarcommons.usf.edu/mhlp_facpub/492/

Geary, P. (2013). Juvenile mental health courts and therapeutic jurisprudence: Facing the challenges posed by youth with mental disabilities in the juvenile justice system. *Yale Journal of Health Policy, Law, and Ethics, 5*(2), 671–710. Retrieved from http://digitalcommons.law.yale.edu/yjhple/vol5/iss2/3

Gralinski-Bakker, J. H., Hauser, S. T., Billings, R. L., & Allen, J. P. (2005). Risks along the road to adulthood: Challenges faced by youth with serious mental disorders. In D. W. Osgood, E. M. Foster, C. Flanagan, & G. R. Ruth (Eds.), *On your own without a net: The transition to adulthood for vulnerable populations* (pp. 272–303). Chicago, IL: The University of Chicago Press.

Herz, D., Lee, P., Lutz, L., Stewart, M., Tuell, J., & Wiig, J. (2012). *Addressing the needs of multi-system youth: Strengthening the connection between child welfare and juvenile justice.* Washington, DC: The Center for Juvenile Justice Reform, Georgetown University, and Robert F. Kennedy Children's Action Corps. Retrieved from http://cjjr.georgetown.edu/pdfs/msy/AddressingtheNeedsofMultiSystemYouth.pdf

Howden, L. M., & Meyer, J. A. (2010). *Age and sex composition: 2010.* Washington, DC: U.S. Census Bureau. Retrieved from http://www.census.gov/prod/cen2010/briefs/c2010br-03.pdf

Hudson, B. (2006). Making and missing connections: Learning disability services and the transition from adolescence to adulthood. *Disability & Society, 21*(1), 47–60.

Johnson, N., Oliff, P., & Williams, E. (2011). *An update on state budget cuts: At least 46 states have imposed cuts that hurt vulnerable residents and cause job loss.* Washington, DC: Center on Budget and Policy Priorities (Updated February 9). Retrieved from http://www.cbpp.org/files/3-13-08sfp.pdf

Jones, V., Dohrn, E., & Dunn, C. (2004). *Creating effective programs for students with emotional and behavior disorders: Interdisciplinary approaches for adding meaning and hope to behavior change interventions.* Boston, MA: Pearson Education.

Levitt, L. (2010). The comparative risk of mistreatment for juveniles in detention facilities and state prisons. *International Journal of Forensic Mental Health, 9*(1), 44–54.

Marsh, S. C., Evans, W. P., & Williams, M. J. (2010). Social support and sense of program belonging discriminate between youth-staff relationship types in juvenile correction settings. *Child & Youth Care Forum, 39*(6), 481–494.

McConkey, R., Kelly, F., Mannan, H., & Craig, S. (2010). Inequalities in respite service provision: Insights from a national, longitudinal study of people with intellectual disabilities. *Journal of Applied Research in Intellectual Disabilities, 23*(1), 85–94.

McMillen, J. C., Zima, B. T., Scott, L. D., Auslander, W. F., Munson, M. R., Ollie, M. T., & Spitznagel, E. L. (2005). Prevalence of psychiatric disorders among older youths in the foster care system. *Journal of the American Academy of Child & Adolescent Psychiatry, 44*(1), 88–95.

Moses, T. (2010). Being treated differently: Stigma experiences with family, peers, and school staff among adolescents with mental health disorders. *Social Science & Medicine, 70*(7), 985–993.

Murray, J., Farrington, D. P., & Sekol, I. (2012). Children's antisocial behavior, mental health, drug use, and educational performance after parental incarceration: A systematic review and meta-analysis. *Psychological Bulletin, 138*(2), 175–210.

Neutens, T., Schwanen, T., Witlox, F., & De Maeyer, P. (2010). Equity of urban service delivery: A comparison of different accessibility measures. *Environment and Planning, 42*(7), 1613–1635.

Ng, I. Y. H., Sarri, R. C., Shook, J. J., & Stoffregen, E. (2012). Comparison of correctional services for youth incarcerated in adult and juvenile facilities in Michigan. *The Prison Journal*, 92(4), 460–483.

Nguyen, H., & Bouchard, M. (2013). Need, connections, or competence? Criminal achievement among adolescent offenders. *Justice Quarterly*, 30(1), 44–83.

Organization for Economic Cooperation and Development (OECD). (2006). *ICT and learning: Supporting out-of-school youth and adults*. Paris, France: Author.

Osgood, D. W., Foster, E. M., & Courtney, M. E. (2010). Vulnerable populations and the transition to adulthood. *The Future of Children*, 20(1), 209–229.

Osgood, D. W., Foster, E. M., Flanagan, C., & Ruth, G. R. (2005). Introduction: Why focus on the transition to adulthood for vulnerable populations? In D. W. Osgood, E. M. Foster, C. Flanagan, & G. R. Ruth (Eds.), *On your own without a net: The transition to adulthood for vulnerable populations* (pp. 1–26). Chicago, IL: The University of Chicago Press.

Puzzanchera, C., Adams, B., & Hockenberry, S. (2012). *Juvenile court statistics 2009*. Pittsburgh, PA: National Center for Juvenile Justice. Retrieved from http://www.ncjj.org/pdf/jcsreports/jcs2009.pdf

Sander, J. B., Sharkey, J. D., Groomes, A. N., Krumholz, L., Walker, K., & Hsu, J. Y. (2011). Social justice and juvenile offenders: Examples of fairness, respect, and access in education settings. *Journal of Educational and Psychological Consultation*, 21(4), 309–337.

Singh, S. P. (2009). Transition of care from child to adult mental health services: The great divide. *Current Opinion in Psychiatry*, 22(4), 386–390.

Sullivan, M. J., Jones, L., & Mathiesen, S. (2010). School change, academic progress, and behavior problems in a sample of foster youth. *Children and Youth Services Review*, 32(2), 164–170.

Transitional Age Youth San Francisco (TAYSF). (2007). *Disconnected youth in San Francisco: A roadmap to improve the life chances of San Francisco's most vulnerable young adults*. San Francisco, CA: Author. Retrieved from http://www.taysf.org/wp-content/uploads/2013/02/TYTF-final-report.pdf

van Uden, J. M., Ritzen, H., & Pieters, J. M. (2014). Engaging students: The role of teacher beliefs and interpersonal teacher behavior in fostering student engagement in vocational education. *Teaching and Teacher Education*, 37, 21–32.

Wagner, M. M. (1995). Outcomes for youths with serious emotional disturbance in secondary school and early adulthood. *The Future of Children*, 5(2), 90–112.

Wagner, M., & Newman, L. (2012). Longitudinal transition outcomes of youth with emotional disturbances. *Psychiatric Rehabilitation Journal*, 35(3), 199–208.

Walsh, L., Lemon, B., Black, R., Mangan, C., & Collin, P. (2011). *The role of technology in engaging disengaged youth: Final report*. Melbourne, Australia: The Foundation of Young Australians. Retrieved from http://www.fya.org.au/app/theme/default/design/assets/publications/Final-Report-AFLF-280411.pdf

Wlodkowski, R. J. (2011). *Enhancing adult motivation to learn: A comprehensive guide for teaching all adults*. San Francisco, CA: Wiley.

RONGBING XIE is a doctoral candidate in the Department of Health Care Organization and Policy, School of Public Health, and serves as a program coordinator for the South Central Preparedness and Emergency Response Learning Center and the Alabama Public Health Training Center at The University of Alabama at Birmingham.

BISAKHA (PIA) SEN is a professor in the Department of Health Care Organization and Policy at The University of Alabama at Birmingham School of Public Health.

E. MICHAEL FOSTER was a professor in the Department of Health Care Organization and Policy at The University of Alabama at Birmingham School of Public Health.

4

This chapter focuses on the transitional experiences of youth with dis/ability labels and highlights how a critical orientation to dis/ability can inform adult educators.

Young Adulthood, Transitions, and Dis/ability

Jessica Nina Lester

For well over three decades, researchers have explored the challenges that youth with dis/ability labels[1] face when transitioning to adult roles (see, e.g., Cheney & Bullis, 2004). While the transition to adulthood has historically been associated with social indicators such as living independently and attending postsecondary school (Keller, Cusick, & Courtney, 2007), not all youth with dis/ability labels (or anyone for that matter) have experienced these events in a predictable manner. In fact, some youth with dis/ability labels are not afforded the opportunity to access or even experience adult responsibilities, highlighting the reality that this particular identity marker (i.e., dis/ability) often "diminishes opportunities for work, education, and leisure" (Rocco & Delgado, 2011, p. 4). As such, it is critical for adult educators working with adults with dis/ability to examine how social and institutional structures might act to facilitate or impede meaningful transitions for youth with dis/ability labels.

The purpose of this chapter is to examine how adult educators might reframe dis/ability as being situated at the nexus of biology and culture, while also recognizing the tangible ways that they can offer support to youth with dis/ability labels. To achieve this aim, I begin the chapter with a brief overview of the national trends and key policies and mandates that frame the transitional process for youth with dis/ability labels in the United States. Then, I discuss briefly how the majority of adult education literature has situated the discussion of youth with dis/ability labels, highlighting the need for a more critical orientation to dis/ability. Next, I present how a social-relational model of dis/ability (Thomas, 1999, 2004) might inform how adult educators make sense of and work with dis/abled youth. Finally, I conclude by sharing practical suggestions for adult educators working with youth with dis/ability labels.

NEW DIRECTIONS FOR ADULT AND CONTINUING EDUCATION, no. 143, Fall 2014 © 2014 Wiley Periodicals, Inc.
Published online in Wiley Online Library (wileyonlinelibrary.com) • DOI: 10.1002/ace.20103

The National Landscape: Youth With Dis/ability Labels in the United States

In the United States, approximately 20% of the adult population identifies as dis/abled (Centers for Disease Control and Prevention [CDC], 2009). While it was notably difficult to define "dis/ability" on a survey, the U.S. Census Bureau (2010a, 2010b) found that 56.7 million people in 2010 identified as dis/abled, with 10.2% of young adults, aged 15–24, identifying as dis/abled. Further, among the young adults included in this age group (i.e., 15–24), 5.3% reported having a severe dis/ability and 1.4% reported needing some kind of assistance.

The National Longitudinal Study-2 was one of the most comprehensive studies of the experiences of secondary students' transition through their early adult years (Sanford et al., 2011). This 10-year study included interviews with youth with dis/ability labels and their parents, as well as surveys. More than 11,000 students receiving special education in at least one grade from 7th to 12th were invited to participate in the study. Over the course of the study, outcomes related to postsecondary education, employment, residential and financial independence, and social and community involvement were examined for those youth who had been out of high school for up to six years.

Some of the findings included young adults with dis/ability labels being: (a) less likely to enroll in postsecondary school than their same-aged peers and (b) less likely to enroll in four-year colleges compared to their same-aged peers. Further, with postsecondary education noted as a primary post–high school goal for more than four out of five secondary students with dis/ability labels (Cameto, Levine, & Wagner, 2004), it is important to note that even when high school programs prepared students with dis/ability labels for postsecondary education, many students still encountered challenges in transitioning from secondary to postsecondary school (Wagner, Newman, & Cameto, 2004). Whether or not youth with dis/ability labels attended postsecondary school varied based on their dis/ability category. For instance, young adults with hearing or visual impairments were more likely to attend postsecondary schools compared to those with autism labels (Sanford et al., 2011).

Full-time employment has been associated with financial and residential independence, and it is viewed as an important step toward "adulthood" for youth with dis/ability labels (Janus, 2009). Yet, it has been well established that compared to the rest of the population, people with dis/ability labels have a higher rate of unemployment (National Collaborative on Workforce & Disability for Youth and Workforce Strategy Center, 2009), and thereby decreased opportunities to live independently. In the longitudinal study conducted by Sanford et al. (2011), while 71% of youth with dis/ability labels reported having a paid job, they earned significantly less than their same-aged peers, while their employment status also varied widely according to their disability category (e.g., 30% of youth with deaf-blindness labels were employed, while 79% of youth with learning dis/ability labels were employed). Overall, from 2005 to

2006, 56.6% of students with dis/ability labels graduated with a high school diploma (American Psychological Association, 2012). Of those who did not graduate, 44.9% had emotional–behavioral disorder labels, 22.7% had speech or language dis/ability labels, 25.1% had learning dis/ability labels, 22.3% had intellectual dis/ability labels, and 23.4% had other health impairment labels (American Psychological Association, 2012).

Notably, then, for adult educators, working with youth with dis/ability labels in a variety of educational contexts (e.g., GED classes, workforce training, university) will likely ensue. As such, it is critical for adult educators to be familiar with the policies and programs that shape how youth with dis/ability labels experience transitions.

Key Policies Supporting Transitions for Youth With Dis/ability Labels

Over the last few decades, public policies related to youth with dis/ability labels have changed significantly (Wittenburg, Golden, & Fishman, 2002). The 1970s and 1980s focused on the "integration" of students with dis/ability labels into "regular" public school classrooms through the development and use of individualized education programs (IEPs). In the 1990s, the focus shifted to developing systems and services to support the transitions of youth with dis/ability labels. For instance, the Americans with Disabilities Act in 1990 resulted in a greater focus on creating equal access to employment for people with dis/ability labels. Also, the amendments made to the Individuals with Disabilities Education Act (IDEA) in 1997 placed a greater emphasis on transition outcomes and community partnerships that lead to employment opportunities for youth with dis/ability labels. Yet, despite many of these important and positive initiatives, policies and the related services have often been experienced as fragmented and imbued with conflicting regulations (Committee on Disability in America, 2007; Rusch & Chadsery, 1998; Stewart et al., 2010, 2013). While there is literature indicating that legislative mandates have had a positive impact, more recent research has highlighted the insufficiency of those policies focused on transition outcomes of youth with dis/ability labels. Many of these policies are written for specific purposes (i.e., education or health) and fail to attend to the abstract nature of transitions.

While research has found that youth with dis/ability labels have similar goals and aspirations as their peers without dis/ability labels (Burchardt, 2004), Stewart et al. (2013) noted a gap between their aspirations and outcomes. Despite the incongruence between policy goals and implementation realities, there are several key policies that impact the day-to-day lives of youth with dis/ability labels. The 2004 reauthorization of IDEA, for instance, has resulted in a greater emphasis being placed on holding schools and states more accountable for post–high school transition outcomes. Other policies that shape the experiences of youth include the American with Disabilities Act

Table 4.1. Key Policies Impacting Transitions for Youth With Dis/ability Labels

Policy	Purpose and Description
Individuals with Disabilities Education Act (IDEA)	This is the primary special education law in the United States. This law guides how states and school districts provide intervention and related services to individuals with dis/ability labels from infancy to age 21.
Section 504 of the Rehabilitation Act	This particular law existed prior to IDEA, as it was part of the civil rights law that prohibited discrimination on the basis of disability. Section 504 assures that individuals with dis/ability labels have equal access to education.
Americans with Disabilities Act (ADA)	This was one of the most comprehensive acts that established equality for people with dis/ability labels. Specifically, this law protects the civil rights of people with dis/ability labels in employment, transportation, and public facility contexts.

(ADA), Assistive Technology Act, and Section 504 of the Rehabilitation Act, to name a few. Table 4.1 provides a brief description of some of these key laws.

Transitions are also supported by both school and nonschool programs (Wittenburg et al., 2002), and include such programs as individualized education programs (i.e., mandated by IDEA), cash assistance programs (e.g., Supplemental Security Income), health insurance programs (e.g., Medicaid), and vocational support programs (e.g., Vocational Rehabilitation program). Several nationwide programs are also in place, all of which seek to create successful transition outcomes. Table 4.2 provides a sampling of some of the resources available specific to employment for youth with dis/ability labels.

While a fairly significant number of policies and programs are in place, relatively little research has examined how youth and adult community members (including educators and employers) view and make sense of such mandates. This dearth of research is particularly true when examining adult education, which is discussed next.

A Brief Consideration of the Literature

Much of the research on transitions of youth with dis/ability labels has been conceptual and/or descriptive in scope (Stewart et al., 2013), with the majority being steeped in traditional understandings of dis/ability. The bulk of this research has been situated in the field of special education and rehabilitation and has focused on barriers to transitioning. Such "barriers" are typically defined in relation to accessing services or systems. Thus, little attention has been given to how youth take up and/or resist new roles as they transition.

More specifically, adult education literature has explored a variety of issues related to dis/ability, including: how people with dis/ability labels make sense of their status (Baumgartner, 2002, 2005; Baumgartner & David, 2009; Courtenay, Merriam, & Reeves, 1998; Courtenay, Merriam, Reeves, &

New Directions for Adult and Continuing Education • DOI: 10.1002/ace

Table 4.2. Resources for Supporting the Transition of Youth With Dis/ability Labels

Organization	Purpose and Description	Website
Department of Vocational Rehabilitation (VR)	This is a federal–state program designed to assist people with dis/ability labels with employment. Each state has a primary VR agency, with local offices located throughout most states.	Each state typically has its own website (e.g., http://www.rehab.cahwnet.gov/).
Job Accommodation Network (JAN)	JAN is a free resource that offers advice and guidance focused on accommodations and employment for individuals with dis/ability labels.	http://askjan.org/
National Center on Workforce and Disability/Adult (NCWD)	The NCWD offers training and other types of assistance aimed at improving the access of workforce systems.	http://www.onestops.info/
Access Board (AB)	AB ensures access to federally funded facilities. If there are concerns regarding accessibility of a federally funded facility, a complaint can be submitted to the AB.	http://www.access-board.gov/the-board

Baumgartner, 2000), the learning experiences inherent to parenting a child with a dis/ability label (Hill, 2001), and the process of sharing one's disability status with others (Rocco, 2001). Beyond this empirical work, there has been some writing around teaching strategies for working with individuals with dis/ability labels in adult education contexts (Covington, 2004; Gadbow, 2001, 2002; Haddad, 1995). Similar to other fields (such as special education), much of the writing in adult education has oriented to dis/ability from a medical or functional perspective (Rocco & Delgado, 2011). From this viewpoint, dis/ability is often presumed to be a deficit or anomaly.

In contrast, the field of disability studies has offered a new orientation to dis/ability, as well as a growing body of empirical work situated within this perspective. From a disability studies perspective, dis/ability is always already a social, cultural, and political phenomenon. This orientation moves the conversation well beyond positioning the dis/abled state as just there (Linton, 1998). Rather than taking up a medical or therapeutic orientation to dis/ability, disability studies scholars reject the idea that a dis/ability is something that must be "fixed." Much of the writing within this interdisciplinary field has provided nuanced and detailed personal accounts of people with dis/ability labels (e.g., Biklen et al., 2005), including youth who are transitioning to "adult" roles.

Overall, there is a need for more research around the transitions of youth with dis/ability labels (Stewart et al., 2013). For instance, to date, little attention has been given to the perceptions and role of adult educators during the transitional process of youth with dis/ability labels. Moreover, there remains a need to examine the everyday experiences of youth with dis/ability labels at the intersection of adult education and a need to develop a more critical orientation to dis/ability. As such, the next section highlights ways of reframing dis/ability from a more socially, culturally, and politically informed perspective.

Reframing Dis/ability in Adult Education

Rocco and Delgado (2011) offered a critique of how adult educators have discussed disabilities. They argued that disability should be a particular concern for a variety of reasons, including that increasing numbers of students with dis/ability labels had begun to enroll in adult and higher education classes. They further noted that few adult educators situated their understanding of disability within a critical theory lens. Rather there is a tendency to orient to dis/ability as different from identity markers such as race, gender, and class—many of which have been framed as socially constructed in the adult education literature. The field has not been quick to position dis/ability as socially and culturally bound. Belzer and Ross-Gordon (2011) have noted that disability is an identity marker that significantly limits one's opportunities for employment, schooling, and social and community engagement. As such, it is critical that adult educators working with youth with dis/ability labels carry with them a nuanced understanding of this complex category, particularly as they seek to ally with youth to coconstruct successful transitions. Drawing upon the work

New Directions for Adult and Continuing Education • DOI: 10.1002/ace

of Thomas (1999, 2004), I next explore the distinctions between the construct of dis/ability and impairment effects, and offer what I consider a more critical view of dis/ability.

A Social-Relational Model of Dis/ability

Within the social-relational model of dis/ability, Thomas (2004) described dis/ability as being created when restrictions were placed on the activities of people labeled dis/abled. The three major components of the social-relational model are: (a) *barriers to being*: behaviors, thoughts, and/or comments that have a negative effect on an individual's sense of self; (b) *barriers to doing*: physical, economic, and material barriers that restrict or prevent people from doing particular activities; and (c) *impairment effects*: restrictions of activity that result from living with an impairment. Specifically, this perspective posits that *impairment effects* and *dis/ability* are interactively experienced by individuals, with both components merging together. For instance, a young adult with a dis/ability label may express herself nonverbally, with this communication defined by some as an *impairment effect*. Yet, the individual's mode of communication is marked as a dis/ability only if it becomes "the marker for other restrictions of activity which do constitute disability" (Thomas, 1999, p. 43). For example, if the nonverbal mode of communication results in her not being allowed to access postsecondary schooling, then a dis/ability emerges. In other words, when people in positions of privilege define how the individual may or may not perform and engage in particular activities due to their impairment, the individual experiences a dis/ability as her rights are denied.

Within this framework, dis/ability is viewed as a social construct, as well as a "form of oppression involving the social imposition of restrictions of activity on people with impairments and the socially engendered undermining of their psycho-emotional wellbeing" (Thomas, 1999, p. 60). With dis/ability only coming into play when there is a restriction placed on one's activities, Thomas (2004) suggested "that it is entirely possible to acknowledge that impairments and chronic illness [may] directly cause *some* restrictions of activity—but such non-socially imposed restrictions of activity do not constitute 'disability'" (p. 581).

How then might such a framework inform how adult educators ally with youth with dis/ability labels? Specifically, as youth experience transitions, it is critical that others find ways to collaborate with them to assure that the established physical and social environments act to support versus impede their participation. Some of the approaches to and important considerations for supporting youth are discussed next.

Supporting Youth With Dis/ability Labels

The final section offers some suggestions for those working with young adults with dis/ability labels. I share four considerations or ways of being, positioning this "list" in relation to critical understandings of dis/ability. Throughout, I presume that working against barriers to being and barriers to doing is a social responsibility and requires each of us to respond in thoughtful ways. This list aims to highlight a few places to begin when working and living with youth with dis/ability labels.

Begin With Relationship. McLean (2011) argued that being in relationship with people with dis/ability labels strengthens one's understanding of the varied meanings of and everyday experiences with dis/ability. She further noted that *kinship* or friendship is key. People who are in consistent relationship with individuals with dis/ability labels come to make sense of dis/ability in new ways, and often seek to collaborate in pursuing new policies and practices that support transitions. This relational perspective is one that is imbued with opportunity for all involved to learn and grow, which will likely result in creating opportunities for transitional experiences to be meaningful and positive.

Assume Competence. Quite often, people with dis/abilities have lived in a world in which others have consistently assumed they are inept or incompetent (e.g., Rentenbach, 2009). Hahn (1986) highlighted how many adults with dis/ability labels were "assumed to be helpless, dependent, asexual, economically unproductive, physically limited, emotionally immature, and acceptable only when they are unobtrusive," thereby allowing others to "act as protectors, guides, leaders, role models, and intermediaries for disabled individuals" (p. 130). Rather than taking up a position that presumed incompetence, Donnellan (1984) argued for presuming competence. She suggested that it was important to always use "the criterion of least dangerous assumption" when being, working, and living with individuals with dis/ability labels (p. 148). This criterion "...holds that we should assume that poor performance is due to instructional inadequacy rather than to student deficits" (p. 147). Thus, the least dangerous assumption calls us to assume that youth with dis/ability labels are competent, able to learn and participate in postsecondary education, capable of acquiring a job, and have aspirations and goals that they can achieve.

Be Open to Learning. There are a multitude of resources available to those committed to working *with* youth with dis/ability labels. From autobiographical accounts to teaching manuals to legal descriptions of policies and programs supporting transitions, adult educators can access materials to support their work with youth. These resources range from specific reports about working with adults with dis/ability labels (Taymans et al., 2009) to books and articles designed to guide adult educators as they think about helpful ways to support youth (Connor, 2012). Being open to learning new ideas and perspectives about the meaning of dis/ability will result in opportunities for meaningful relationships with youth, and increased support through their transitions.

Be an Ally. Allies are individuals who recognize their privilege and how that privilege affords them access to certain economic, social, and political institutions; yet, allies do not simply recognize their privilege, they work against patterns of injustice (Bishop, 2002). In the case of youth with dis/ability labels, an ally is one who recognizes that ableism, "discrimination on the grounds that being able bodied is the normal and superior human condition" (McLean, 2011, p. 13), is alive and well, and therefore requires all of us to continually work against institutional inequities. While policies and programs specific to transitions for youth with dis/ability labels have made some positive impact, inequities still exist and demand that allies respond by collaborating and joining with youth to resist and shift barriers to being and doing.

Conclusions

The transition to adulthood for youth with dis/ability labels requires careful attention to policies and programs that have an impact on the transitional process. It is equally important to attend to the social, cultural, and political environments that sustain inequitable access to employment, postsecondary education, and independent living for youth. By taking a more critical orientation to dis/ability—specifically one that acknowledges impairment effects, barriers to being, and barriers to doing—adult educators can more effectively and meaningfully ally with youth in a joint pursuit of positive transition outcomes.

Note

1. Writing about people's identities is a fragile task, as language always has consequence (whether intended or not). When deciding whether to use person first language (e.g., adult with disability), I considered the writing of Broderick and Ne'eman (2008) who suggested that naming individuals with dis/ability labels as people first (e.g., woman with intellectual dis/ability) might actually result in reifying the "impairment" (e.g., intellectual dis/ability) as a tangible reality. Recognizing that dis/ability is always already socially and culturally embedded and is something that is developed (not discovered), throughout this chapter, I used phrases such as "youth with dis/ability labels" or "dis/abled youth" with caution. Further, I chose to separate the "dis" from the "ability" to emphasize the assumption that ability is central to my orientation to individuals who are labeled and/or identify as dis/abled.

References

American Psychological Association. (2012). *Facing the school dropout dilemma*. Washington, DC: Author. Retrieved from http://www.apa.org/pi/families/resources/school-dropout-prevention.aspx

Baumgartner, L. M. (2002). Living and learning with HIV/AIDS: Transformational tales continued. *Adult Education Quarterly, 53*(1), 44–59.

Baumgartner, L. M. (2005). HIV-positive adults' meaning making over time. In J. Egan (Ed.), *New Directions for Adult and Continuing Education: No. 105. HIV/AIDS sourcebook* (pp. 11–20). San Francisco, CA: Jossey-Bass.

Baumgartner, L. M., & David, K. N. (2009, May). PoZitively transformative: The transformative learning of people living with HIV. Proceedings of the 50th Annual Adult Education Research Conference, National-Louis University, Louisville, KY.

Belzer, A., & Ross-Gordon, J. (2011). Revisiting debates on learning disabilities in adult education. In T. S. Rocco (Ed.), *New Directions for Adult and Continuing Education: No. 132. Challenging ableism, understanding disability, including adults with disabilities in workplaces and learning spaces* (pp. 75–101). San Francisco, CA: Jossey-Bass.

Biklen, D., Attfield, R., Bissonnette, L., Blackman, L., Burke, J., Frugone, A., ... Rubin, S. (2005). *Autism and the myth of the person alone*. New York: New York University Press.

Bishop, A. (2002). *On becoming an ally: Breaking the cycle of oppression in people* (2nd ed.). London, UK: Zed Books.

Broderick, A. A., & Ne'eman, A. (2008). Autism as metaphor: Narrative and counter narrative. *International Journal of Inclusive Education, 12*(5–6), 459–476.

Burchardt, T. (2004). Aiming high: The educational and occupational aspirations of young disabled people. *Support for Learning, 19*(4), 181–186.

Cameto, R., Levine, P., & Wagner, M. (2004). *Transition planning for students with disabilities: A special topic report from the National Longitudinal Transition Study-2 (NLTS2)*. Menlo Park, CA: SRI International.

Centers for Disease Control and Prevention (CDC). (2009). *How many people have disabilities?* Atlanta, GA: Author. Retrieved from http://www.cdc.gov/ncbddd/documents /Disability%20tip%20sheet%20_PHPa_1.pdf

Cheney, D., & Bullis, M. (2004). The school-to-community transition of adolescents with emotional and behavioral disorders. In R. B. Rutherford, M. M. Quinn, & S. R. Mathur (Eds.), *Handbook of research in emotional and behavioral disorders* (pp. 369–384). New York, NY: Guilford.

Committee on Disability in America. (2007). Health care transitions for young people. In M. J. Field & A. M. Jette (Eds.), *Future of disability in America* (pp. 98–135). Washington, DC: The National Academies Press.

Connor, D. J. (2012). Helping students with disabilities transition to college: 21 tips for students with LD and/or ADD/ADHD. *Teaching Exceptional Children, 44*(5), 16–25.

Courtenay, B. C., Merriam, S. B., & Reeves, P. M. (1998). The centrality of meaning-making in transformational learning: How HIV-positive adults make sense of their lives. *Adult Education Quarterly, 48*(2), 65–84.

Courtenay, B. C., Merriam, S. B., Reeves, P. M., & Baumgartner, L. (2000). Perspective transformation over time: A 2-year follow-up study of HIV-positive adults. *Adult Education Quarterly, 50*(2), 102–119.

Covington, L. E. (2004). Moving beyond the limits of learning: Implications of learning disabilities for adult education. *Adult Basic Education, 14*(2), 90–103.

Donnellan, A. (1984). The criterion of the least dangerous assumption. *Behavioral Disorders, 9*, 141–150.

Gadbow, N. F. (2001). Teaching strategies that help learners with different needs. *Adult Learning, 12*(2), 19–21.

Gadbow, N. F. (2002). Teaching all learners as if they are special. In J. M. Ross-Gordon (Ed.), *New Directions for Adult and Continuing Education: No. 93. Contemporary viewpoints on teaching adults effectively* (pp. 51–61). San Francisco, CA: Jossey-Bass.

Haddad, P. I. (1995). Teaching the learning-disabled adult. *Adult Learning, 6*(4), 9.

Hahn, H. (1986). Public support for rehabilitation programmes: The analysis of U.S. Disability Policy. *Disability, Handicap and Society, 1*(2), 121–137.

Hill, L. H. (2001). My child has a learning disability, now what? *Adult Learning, 12*(2), 24–25.

Janus, A. L. (2009). Disability and the transition to adulthood. *Social Forces, 88*(1), 99–120.

Keller, T. E., Cusick, G. R., & Courtney, M. E. (2007). Approaching the transition to adulthood: Distinctive profiles of adolescents aging out of the child welfare system. *Social Service Review, 81*(3), 453–484.

Linton, S. (1998). *Claiming disability: Knowledge and identity*. New York: New York University Press.

McLean, M. A. (2011). Getting to know you: The prospect of challenging ableism through adult learning. In T. S. Rocco (Ed.), *New Directions for Adult and Continuing Education: No. 132. Challenging ableism, understanding disability, including adults with disabilities in workplaces and learning spaces* (pp. 13–22). San Francisco, CA: Jossey-Bass.

National Collaborative on Workforce & Disability for Youth and Workforce Strategy Center. (2009). *Career-focused services for students with disabilities at community colleges.* Washington, DC: Institute for Educational Leadership.

Rentenbach, B. (2009). *Synergy.* Bloomington, IN: AuthorHouse.

Rocco, T. S. (2001). Helping adult educators understand disability disclosure. *Adult Learning, 12*(2), 10–12.

Rocco, T. S., & Delgado, A. (2011). Shifting lenses: A critical examination of disability in adult education. In T. S. Rocco (Ed.), *New Directions for Adult and Continuing Education: No. 132. Challenging ableism, understanding disability, including adults with disabilities in workplaces and learning spaces* (pp. 3–12). San Francisco, CA: Jossey-Bass.

Rusch, F., & Chadsery, J. (Eds.). (1998). *Beyond high school: Transition from school to work.* Belmont, CA: Wadsworth.

Sanford, C., Newman, L., Wagner, M., Cameto, R., Knokey, A.-M., & Shaver, D. (2011). *The post-high school outcomes of young adults with disabilities up to 6 years after high school. Key findings from the National Longitudinal Transition Study-2 (NLTS2)* (NCSER 2011-3004). Menlo Park, CA: SRI International.

Stewart, D., Freeman, M., Law, M., Healy, H., Burke-Gaffney, J., Forhan, M., ... Guenther, S. (2010). *The best journey to adult life for youth with disabilities: An evidence-based model and best practice guidelines for the transition to adulthood.* Retrieved from http://transitions.canchild.ca/en/OurResearch/bestpractices.asp

Stewart, D., Freeman, M., Law, M., Healy, H., Burke-Gaffney, J., Forhan, M., ... Guenther, S. (2013). Transition to adulthood for youth with disabilities: Evidence from the literature. In J. H. Stone & M. Blouin (Eds.), *International encyclopedia of rehabilitation.* Retrieved from http://cirrie.buffalo.edu/encyclopedia/en/article/110/

Taymans, J. M., Swanson, H. L., Schwartz, R. L., Gregg, N., Hock, M., & Gerber, P. J. (2009). *Learning to achieve: A review of the research literature on serving adults with learning disabilities.* Washington, DC: National Institute for Literacy.

Thomas, C. (1999). *Female forms: Experiencing and understanding disability.* Buckingham, UK: Open University Press.

Thomas, C. (2004). How is disability understood? An examination of sociological approaches. *Disability & Society, 19*(6), 569–583.

U.S. Census Bureau. (2010a). *Facts for features: Veterans Day 2010: Nov. 11.* Washington, DC: Bureau of the Census.

U.S. Census Bureau. (2010b, May–August). *Survey of income and program participation.* Washington, DC: Bureau of the Census.

Wagner, M., Newman, L., & Cameto, R. (2004). *Changes over time in the secondary school experiences of students with disabilities. A report of findings from the National Longitudinal Transition Study (NLTS) and the National Longitudinal Transition Study-2 (NLTS2).* Menlo Park, CA: SRI International.

Wittenburg, D. C., Golden, T., & Fishman, M. (2002). Transition options for youth with disabilities: An overview of the programs and policies that affect the transition from school. *Journal of Vocational Rehabilitation, 17,* 195–206.

JESSICA NINA LESTER is an assistant professor of inquiry methodology in the Department of Counseling and Educational Psychology at Indiana University.

5

This chapter describes developmental needs of emerging young adults and how they are often met, or not met, in faith communities. The author offers recommendations for creating better connections with today's emerging young adults.

Becoming an Adult in a Community of Faith

Steven B. Frye

In recent years, spirituality and faith development have become vital components in the thinking of theorists interested in adult development (Tisdell, 2008). As Merriam (2008) has aptly stated, "spirituality and its relationship to adult learning and adult education has emerged as a prominent stream of writing and research in the last ten years" (p. 96). With the growing appreciation for the many dimensions of adult learning, spirituality is recognized as "all encompassing and cannot be torn from other aspects of adult development" (Tisdell, 1999, p. 94). This volume's consideration of the transitions from adolescence to adulthood would be incomplete without some attention to these transitions in the context of faith communities. In the United States, faith groups devote great amounts of energy and finances working with youth and college-aged adults, with goals of offering guidance and assistance to young adults through these tumultuous years. In this chapter, I will explore the position that faith communities[1] have in lives of young adults, highlight some of the points that can be gleaned from the work of adult educators working in faith communities, and offer some recommendations that could enhance the work of these faith groups and adult educators in general as they seek to engage the ever-changing young adults of early 2000s.

Young Adults and Organized Religion

The following scenario could be played in many weekly gatherings of religious organizations in the United States. The leaders are preparing for the beginning of worship and the auditorium is busy with children running between their parents' legs, teenagers gathering together in the back row, older adults shaking hands and discussing this past week's events, and young mothers busily planning the next parents' day out gathering. A cursory look would leave one with the impression that this was a pretty balanced group, crossing the spectrum from "cradle to grave." A longer look would reveal something is

NEW DIRECTIONS FOR ADULT AND CONTINUING EDUCATION, no. 143, Fall 2014 © 2014 Wiley Periodicals, Inc.
Published online in Wiley Online Library (wileyonlinelibrary.com) • DOI: 10.1002/ace.20104

missing—where are the young adults? Teenagers, check. Young families with children, check. Older parents and grandparents, check. The young adults seem to be largely absent from the auditorium. Does anyone present even notice they are missing?

Religious organizations tend to emphasize work with adolescents, assisting them through the troublesome years of middle and high school with paid professional youth workers, organized youth groups, focused service and ministry opportunities, and a variety of offerings to build community. The Barna Group (2011), a research organization that specializes in studying religious life in the United States, found that only three in 10 young adults who were active in congregational life as teenagers remained active through the vitally important developmental period of their twenties. Among Jewish congregations, only 12% of Jewish congregation members are in their twenties at the end of the 20th century (Wuthnow, 2007, p. 74). While congregations spend significant effort in supporting the teenage faithful, one glaring question remains: What about the post–high school years?

Faith Development

The transition from youth to young adulthood is one filled with uncertainty. This move has long been the focus of developmental theorists like Piaget and Erikson, and it continues to be a priority of educators who work with emerging adults. What does it mean to become "adult" and how can this transition be facilitated within a community of faith?

One of the most influential theorists dealing with spiritual development is James Fowler. In his book *Stages of Faith*, Fowler (1981) developed a model for the stages humans traverse as they grow into mature adult faith. He proposed a six-stage comprehensive system that describes the process of spiritual development from childhood through adulthood. Fowler's second stage describes the faith of school-age children as *mythic-literal faith*. As the name implies, symbols and interpretations of truth are highly literal and not reflective. In stage three, *synthetic/conventional faith* (adolescence and beyond), authority is found outside of the individual and accepted as true. At this stage, "one's ideology or worldview is lived and asserted; it is not yet a matter of critical reflection and articulation" (Fowler, 1996, p. 61). In the fourth stage, *individuative–reflective faith* (young adulthood and beyond), authority moves from external to internal. Old assumptions are reexamined and responsibility is taken in a new way. The individual moves away from being defined by the group, and relationships are chosen based on self-authored beliefs or values. There is a move away from self-preoccupation in stage five, *conjunctive faith* (midlife and beyond). In this stage, there is a search for balance, and alternate conceptions of truth are acknowledged to exist and have validity. In this stage, another person's conceptions of truths may be valid and true "for them." This often leads to tolerance for others and activity in service and commitment to others. In this stage, the individual struggles with the notion of universality, while at the

New Directions for Adult and Continuing Education • DOI: 10.1002/ace

same time maintaining individuality. Fowler's system has a final stage of faith, *universalizing faith* (midlife and beyond) that he considers a rare achievement. Here, there is a step beyond individuality toward the external, and absolute love and justice are lived. Life is immersed into others.

As a student of Fowler and a specialist in young adult spiritual development, Sharon Daloz Parks (2000) added to Fowler's work by focusing on transitions that occur throughout young adulthood. She described the spiritual development process from adolescence through adulthood in four parts:

1. *Adolescent/conventional—authority bound* (accepts the conventions of the group and social norms) and *counterdependent* (pushing against yet still authority bound).
2. *Young adult—probing commitment.* A time of fragile inner-dependence (like a young plant): "healthy, vital, full of promise, yet vulnerable" (p. 82).
3. *Tested adult—confident inner-dependence.* The tested adult is "able self-consciously to include self within the arena of authority" (p. 77). Inner-dialogue is vital as the adult begins to listen within. Mentors become peers and authority becomes "fully equilibrated within" (p. 88).
4. *Mature adult—interdependent faith.* A dialectic faith where dialogue is not only merely "expedient but essential." The mature adult "can depend upon others without fear of losing the self" (p. 87).

Parks, like Fowler, emphasized the probing of commitments. During this time of transition, burgeoning young adults test the spiritual concepts and commitments of adolescence. External belief structures develop to inner beliefs, and these beliefs are sifted and self-tested. Although some significant questions remain about the universal applicability of these stage-based approaches of Fowler and Parks (e.g., applications outside of Western cultures, cognitive focus, emphasis on individuality rather than social construction), they "represent the most thorough investigations to date into how individuals develop their religious and spiritual attitudes and beliefs" (Chickering, Dalton, & Stamm, 2006, pp. 63–64).

Who Are Today's Young Adults?

Modern developmental theorists acknowledge the unique nature of generations in U.S. society. According to Kinnaman (2011), a generation "reflects the idea that people who are born during a certain period of time are influenced by the unique set of circumstances and global events, moral and social values, technologies, and cultural and behavioral norms" (p. 246). The rapid societal and technological changes that have occurred over the past 50+ years have resulted in marked differences between generations. The Barna Group (2011) identified the four most recent generations as follows:

New Directions for Adult and Continuing Education • DOI: 10.1002/ace

1. *Mosaics* (1984–2002): The Barna Group uses the term *Mosaics* "because it reflects their eclectic relationships, thinking styles, and learning formats, among other things" (Kinnaman, 2011, p. 246). Also referred to as Generation Y or Millennials.
2. *Busters* (1965–1983): Often referred to as Generation X.
3. *Boomers* (1946–1964): The post-WWII generation.
4. *Elders* (pre-1946): Called the "greatest generation" or "builders."

Although every new generation has had marked differences from the preceding generation, the Millennials grew up in a time of rapid and unprecedented technological advancement, including the proliferation of digital media and the normalization of social media. For many in this generation, information has always been easily accessible, multiple cultures have always been visible in media, the definition of family has been ever-changing, and public and religious authority has always been questioned in the public sphere. As Kinnaman (2011) so aptly stated regarding the latest generation, they come at life as a mosaic, borrowing from multiple belief structures and appreciating the varied ethnic landscape.

Religious Involvement of Young Adults

Even with the widespread practice of emphasizing youth ministries, the number of young adults who do not identify themselves with any religious group is on the rise. According to the Pew Foundation on Religion and Public Life (2012), during the past five years the number of adults who identify themselves as unaffiliated with any religious group has risen from 15% to 20%. Among young adults the numbers are more pronounced. The Pew study found that one third of adults under age 30 professed no religious affiliation (32%). Among the youngest Millennials, aged 18–22, the number rose to 34%. The gap in the young adult demographic is noticeable; Kinnaman (2011) referred to young adults ages 18–29 as the "black hole of church attendance" (p. 22). Furthermore, 74% of those who identified themselves as unaffiliated were raised with some religious affiliation. Even with the concentrated effort expended by faith groups, there are a growing number of young adults who are uninvolved in faith communities during this transitional period of adult development.

In his book *You Lost Me*, Kinnaman (2011) identified three broad categories of young adults who, although previously having been involved in church, now fall into the category of "lost": (a) "Nomads" who have walked away from church attendance, but still consider themselves Christians (four in 10); (b) "Exiles" who are still involved and invested in the Christian faith, but "feel stuck between culture and church" (two in 10); (c) "Prodigals" who have lost faith and consider themselves as "no longer Christian" (one in 10) (p. 25). It is interesting to note that these young adults who are no longer involved in congregational life as a whole do not have a negative view of spirituality or

New Directions for Adult and Continuing Education • DOI: 10.1002/ace

faith issues. Instead, it is their relationship with congregational life with which they struggle. Kinnaman contended that this alienation can be traced to issues like exclusivity of some religious groups, perceptions that religion and science are at odds, regressive viewpoints of sexuality, little tolerance for doubt and intellectual questioning, and a lack of openness to changes occurring within society.

Robert Wuthnow (2007), a sociologist who commented on the modern decline in church attendance, identified broader social and demographic trends that are helping to precipitate the decline. He noted the postponement of marriage and parenthood by a growing number of young adults. Married adults and those with children are more likely to be regular church attenders. For the single or childless adult in his or her twenties, religious organizations can be perceived as having little relevance. Sam Rainer (2013), researcher and contributor to the Southern Baptist Convention's Lifeway education website, commented that "in the short, four-year transitional window of teen to adult, the church loses the majority of its students" (para. 1). He stated:

> Most of the [church] dropouts do not leave their families during this time. Most of the dropouts do not leave their social networks during this time. Most of the dropouts do not leave the educational system during this time. But most of them leave the church. (Rainer, 2013, para. 2)

What Does Work?

In light of these rather staggering statistics, it is clear that many things about faith communities are not working with the current generation of emerging adults. But for the three in 10, what is working? What characteristics keep these complex individuals involved and maturing in the faith community? Keith (2013) described a grounded theory study conducted in England that sought to examine "emerging practices amongst churches with growing numbers of young adults" (p. 8). The study participants included church groups representing the Church of England, Methodist, Baptist, free churches, new congregations sponsored by the Church Missionary Society and the Church Army, and other independent Christian churches. The following common key values were found among these groups to be successful with young adults: community (the term "family" was frequently used), authenticity ("realness" over "rightness"), openness to doubt (valued rather than discouraged), spirituality (the felt nature of the spiritual encounter), and change (a continuous transition of people) (pp. 12–13).

Mark Putnam (2012), president of Central College in Pella, Iowa, offered three observations:

> ...for those seeking to deepen the relationship between the church and the emerging generation of young adults:

1. Young adults, even those who profess faith, are questioning the church's relevance.
2. When they do encounter the church, they bring increasing expectations of authenticity.
3. Any desire to stay in the church rests on their expanding ideas of community. (pp. 8–9)

Similar themes were discovered by Stetzer, Stanley, and Hayes (2009) when they surveyed young adults and churches successful in reaching young adults. They identified four "markers" for young adult ministry: community (life is experienced together); depth (significance of those experiences); responsibility (actions and choices make a difference); and connection (mentoring, learning from those who have already experienced what they are facing) (pp. 67–68).

Community. The concepts of community and belonging are vital issues for today's emerging young adult generation. Copeland (2012) stated that "as many have noted about young adults today, we tend to seek belonging first; believing comes later" (para. 5). Copeland is the founder of Project F-M, a specialized Lutheran-based ministry for young adults, with the mission of "making space for 20/30-somethings to love God and neighbor by cultivating an open-minded, curious faith" (theprojectfm.org). Ginny Moyer (2005) discussed her experience in a parish-based ministry for Catholic 20- to 30-year-olds:

> Young adult ministry ... has to be about creating a space where anyone can go on a spiritual journey. It has to be about providing a safe place to question, to disagree, to grow. After all, the 20s and 30s are when many lapsed Catholics start, tentatively, to reengage with their childhood faith. Young adult ministry needs to be a door through which these Catholics can enter back into the church. It has to be about welcoming those who have a million reasons not to be there. (p. 12)[2]

Leaders of young adults recognize that community is an essential part of the journey of development, but experiencing authentic community can be made more difficult by the transient lives of many young adults. Naomi Abelson, associate director of Young Adult Engagement for the Union of Reformed Judaism, described efforts to help young adults understand Jewish community as a "movement" rather than isolated "microcosms." This larger concept of community helps to foster a "seamless journey rather than an episodic journey" so that when a young adult moves to another location, he or she might connect with another congregation (N. Abelson, personal communication, September 12, 2013).

Authenticity. The Millennial generation has grown up in a world inundated with advertising. While Boomers and Busters have experienced a vast amount of advertising through television, radio, and print ads, today's emerging young adults are bombarded with ads on social media, cell phone apps,

YouTube videos, and websites. Therefore, they are sensitive to truthfulness and have what Evans (2013) called a healthy "B.S. meter." Beth Ludlum, director of student faith and formation at the United Methodist Board of Higher Education, contends that young adults have "authenticity radar." The newsletter article entitled *Get Real! Young Adults Have Authenticity Radar* recommended that churches strive for authenticity in the following areas: conversation, diversity, hospitality, relationships, topics, and teaching. Successful incorporation of young adults into the life of the congregation will require honest engagement of life issues and real-world problems. This honesty and authenticity are summed up in the article's closing statement: "as we seek to open our hearts, minds and doors to the next generation, we can work to become a more authentic expression of the body of Christ" (United Methodist Communications, 2013, para. 10). A similar theme can be found in Feinberg's (2009) essay in the Assemblies of God publication *Enrichment Journal*. Much of her article *What Twentysomethings Wish You Knew* focuses on this desire for authentic relationships. Among the young adults she interviewed, she found a resounding theme of loneliness, even among married young adults. She recommends caring, honest, and authentic mentoring relationships with older adults.

Spirituality. Many young adults who are not involved in religious communities are interested in spirituality. This concept has been a popular topic in adult learning literature (Isaac, 2012; Tisdell, 2003, 2008). Fowler (1996) defined faith as "a dynamic, evolving pattern of the ways our souls find and make meanings for our lives" (p. 21). Spirituality often has a similar definition in adult education literature, emphasizing the search for meaning (Fleming & Courtenay, 2006; Parks, 2000; Tisdell, 2003). Fenwick and English (2004) identified the trend as an "eclectic" spirituality that is not directly tied to religious sectarianism. Religion is perceived as what one does, and spirituality as what one is (Fowler, 1996). One hopeful note for adult religious educators is that while the unaffiliated are shy of active participation in religious services and activities, they are not wholly "irreligious." Two thirds say they believe in God, and 55% consider themselves as either a "religious person (18%) or as spiritual but not religious (37%)" (Pew Foundation on Religion and Public Life, 2012, p. 22). There is openness on the part of young adults who enter into dialogue about spiritual issues, even those who would consider religious attendance as anathema. Facebook and other social media are often the domain of lively faith discussions between active faith-group participants, vehement nonbelievers (often Kinnaman's "Prodigals"), and seekers. One thing that often stands out in these discussions is the openness that allows each voice a place at the table.

Recommendations for Practice

The following section offers recommendations for common areas of connection for engaging today's emerging young adults and assisting them through significant periods of development. While these recommendations apply directly to the work of religious organizations, the themes have application for adult educators in a multitude of settings.

Create an Atmosphere of Authenticity. The young adults the Barna Group calls "Mosaics" are experts at ferreting out hypocrisy. While they are an open and forgiving group in their relationships, they do not possess the organizational loyalty of earlier generations that will tolerate inauthentic relationships. Charlie Grenade, a minister serving single adults at Dayspring Baptist Church in Mobile, Alabama, commenting on worship experiences said that "one of the trends we're noticing is people are looking for something that's real....College students are looking for a worship service where there's nothing fancy...it's not about the bells and whistles" (Campbell, 2004, p. 16).

Emphasize Experience. This is a generation of doers rather than hearers. It is essential that religious organizations incorporate young adults into the life and leadership of the group. They do not want to hear about what the representatives of the group have done to help others; they want to be part of the solution. *Project Connect*, a program associated with the Evangelical Lutheran Church of America, offers resources to help congregations connect with young adults (projectconnect.org). The congregational resource, *Connect: Calling Leaders for a Changing World*, offers the following statement about young adult participation:

> Young Adult Ministry is more than just having young adults present in your congregation. It is an intentional process of welcoming and involving young adults as full participants and vital members of a congregation. Young adult ministry involves providing an atmosphere in your congregation where young adults (aged 18 to 30) are treated as leaders in the community of faith whose gifts are respected and utilized, and who are integral to a dynamic, active program that aims to help them mature into the people God has called them to be. (Project Connect, 2013, p. 2)

Allow Room for Difference and Doubt. Developmental theorists like Fowler (1996), Parks (1986, 2000), and Kegan (1994) pointed to the need for personal ownership of beliefs as an integral component of mature adult faith. Exploration of alternative concepts is essential in this process of moving from the beliefs of others (inherited beliefs) to personal (self-authored) beliefs. Rachel Held Evans (2013), CNN religion blogger, author, and frequent speaker on religious groups connecting to young adults, speaks to this need for space for doubt in her blog: "I talk about how the evangelical obsession with sex can make Christian living seem like little more than sticking to a list of rules, and how Millennials long for faith communities in which they are safe asking tough questions and wrestling with doubt" (para. 8). The goal is dialogue, what Isaacs (1999) defined as "a conversation with a center, not sides" (p. 19). Meeting the needs of young adult faith development includes space for what 9th-century philosopher and theologian Anselm of Canterbury called

New Directions for Adult and Continuing Education • DOI: 10.1002/ace

"faith seeking understanding" (Stanford Encyclopedia of Philosophy, 2007, section 2.1).

Appreciate the Ever-Changing Concept of Spirituality. The transition from adolescence to young adulthood is a time of identity transformation. Erikson (1968) considered this struggle to be primary "crisis" of adolescence. Marcia (1966) described Identity Moratorium as a time when youth were in the process of searching to find that which best suited them. This trying on of identities is a normal part of the growth process. Applied to faith issues, this quest should be expected to involve searching and questioning. Postmodernism has brought a less religiously confined concept of spirituality that is true to the mosaic nature of today's emerging young adults. Dialogue is valued over dogma, discussion over decrees. This may be one of the strongest challenges in the intergenerational conversations of congregational life. Successful integration of young adults and healthy nurturing of faith will require an appreciation of this application of spirituality.

Discover the Value of Intergenerational Mentoring. Mentoring has long been appreciated as a valid and effective form of education in the field of adult learning (Daloz, 1999). National research on youth and religion found that teenagers who remained active in congregational life in the post-youth years "had a number of adults in their congregations who they could turn to for advice, wisdom, and encouragement" (Black, 2008, p. 41). Mentors serve as guides for the emerging adult, voices of experience that offer hope for young adults struggling to find authentic faith. Parks (1986) contended that mentors "help anchor the vision of the potential self" (p. 81). Those who have successfully navigated the troublesome course of faith development offer veteran advice and experience-based hope to evolving young adults.

Conclusions

Young adult development involves a growth process where authority moves from inherited beliefs and values toward an evolving set of self-authored beliefs and values. Adult learning literature has repeatedly included spirituality as an integral component of this growth. Religious organizations have an important role as adult educators in this developmental process. Current research shows that in spite of intense efforts and energy invested in work with adolescents there is a marked disconnect during the important period between late adolescence and early adulthood. Generational differences, social misunderstandings, and changing definitions of spirituality often build fences rather than bridges, which can leave young adults with little congregational support in the process of moving from inherited faith to self-owned faith. The literature reveals that these young adults seek authenticity, community, and a spirituality connected to the real world that appreciates the ever-changing world they inhabit.

The adult education field as a whole can learn much from the efforts of adult educators who work in faith communities. Educators seeking to engage young adults in academic settings, community organizers, literacy educators, and proponents of popular education all share the task of making connection with emerging young adults. Creating an atmosphere of authenticity, emphasizing experience, allowing room for difference and doubt, connecting to the spiritual components of life and development, and appreciating the benefits of intergenerational mentoring all have application for adult educators in religious communities, as well as in the many other communities that make up the broad field of adult education.

Notes

1. Much of the recent research and writing on young adults and faith communities has focused on Christian groups. Other faith traditions are considered and included when possible.

2. Reprinted by permission of National Catholic Reporter, 115 East Armour Boulevard, Kansas City, MO 64111, USA, www.ncronline.org.

References

Barna Group. (2011). *Five myths about young adult church dropouts*. Retrieved from https: //www.barna.org/barna-update/teens-nextgen/534-five-myths-about-young-adult -church-dropouts#.UeIV7E8Qju0

Black, W. (2008). Stopping the dropouts: Guiding adolescents toward a lasting faith following high school graduation. *Christian Education Journal, 5*(1), 28–46.

Campbell, K. (2004). Young adults missing from the pews. *Christian Century, 121*(3), 16.

Chickering, A. W., Dalton, J. C., & Stamm, L. (2006). *Encouraging authentic spirituality in higher education*. San Francisco, CA: Jossey-Bass.

Copeland, A. J. (2012, May 30). Reaching out to young adults will screw up your church. *The Huffington Post: Religion Blog*. Retrieved from http://www.huffingtonpost.com/rev -adam-j-copeland/reaching-out-to-young-adults-will-screw-up-your-church_b_1543142 .html

Daloz, L. (1999). *Mentor: Guiding the journey of adult learners* (2nd ed.). San Francisco, CA: Jossey-Bass.

Erikson, E. H. (1968). *Identity, youth, and crisis*. New York, NY: W. W. Norton.

Evans, R. H. (2013, July 27). Why millennials are leaving the church. *CNN Belief Blog*. Retrieved from http://religion.blogs.cnn.com/2013/07/27/why-millennials-are-leaving -the-church

Feinberg, M. (2009). What twentysomethings wish you knew. *Enrichment Journal*. Retrieved from http://enrichmentjournal.ag.org/200903/200903_034_Twentysomethng.cfm

Fenwick, T. J., & English, L. M. (2004). Dimensions of spirituality: A framework for adult educators. *Adult Theological Education, 1*(1), 49–64.

Fleming, J. J., & Courtenay, B. C. (2006, June). *The role of spirituality in the practice of adult education leaders*. Proceedings of the 46th Adult Education Research Conference, University of Minnesota, Minneapolis, MN.

Fowler, J. W. (1981). *Stages of faith: The psychology of human development and the quest for meaning*. San Francisco, CA: Harper & Row.

Fowler, J. W. (1996). *Faithful change: The personal and public challenges of postmodern life*. Nashville, TN: Abingdon.

Isaac, E. P. (Ed.). (2012). *New Directions for Adult and Continuing Education: No. 133. Expanding the boundaries of adult religious education: Strategies, techniques, and partnerships for the new millennium*. San Francisco, CA: Jossey-Bass.

Isaacs, W. (1999). *Dialogue and the art of thinking together*. New York, NY: Currency.

Kegan, R. (1994). *In over our heads: The mental demands of modern life*. Cambridge, MA: Harvard University Press.

Keith, B. (2013). *Authentic faith: Fresh expressions of church amongst young adults*. London, UK: Fresh Expressions.

Kinnaman, D. (2011). *You lost me: Why young Christians are leaving the church and rethinking faith*. Grand Rapids, MI: Baker Books.

Marcia, J. E. (1966). Development and validation of ego-identity status. *Journal of Personality and Social Psychology, 3*, 551–558.

Merriam, S. B. (2008). Adult learning theory for the twenty-first century. In S. B. Merriam (Ed.), *New Directions for Adult and Continuing Education: No. 119. Third update on adult learning theory* (pp. 93–98). San Francisco, CA: Jossey-Bass.

Moyer, G. (2005). Young adults: Dialog across the divide. *National Catholic Reporter, 41*(40), 12.

Parks, S. D. (1986). *The critical years: The young adult search for a faith to live by*. San Francisco, CA: Harper & Row.

Parks, S. D. (2000). *Big questions worthy dreams: Mentoring young adults in their search for meaning, purpose, and faith*. San Francisco, CA: Jossey-Bass.

Pew Foundation on Religion and Public Life. (2012). *"Nones" on the rise: One in five adults have no religious affiliation*. Washington, DC: Pew Research Center.

Project Connect. (2013). *Connect: Calling leaders for a changing world* [Congregational Resource Packet]. A project of the Eastern Cluster of Lutheran Seminaries funded by Lilly Endowment, Inc. Retrieved from http://projectconnect.org/images/uploads/connecting-young-adults-with-ministries.pdf

Putnam, M. (2012). The search for authentic, relevant community: The journey of young adults. *Perspectives: A Journal of Reformed Thought, 2012*(9), 8–10. Retrieved from http://www.rca.org/page.aspx?pid=8925

Rainer, S. (2013, June 4). *Four keys to keeping young adults in church. Lifeway: Articles*. Retrieved from http://www.lifeway.com/Article/four-keys-to-keeping-young-adults

Stanford Encyclopedia of Philosophy. (2007). *Saint Anselm*. Retrieved from http://plato.stanford.edu/entries/anselm/

Stetzer, E., Stanley, R., & Hayes, J. (2009). *Lost and found: The younger unchurched and the churches that reach them*. Nashville, TN: B & H Publishing.

Tisdell, E. J. (1999). The spiritual dimension of adult development. In M. C. Clark & R. S. Caffarella (Eds.), *New Directions for Adult and Continuing Education: No. 84. An update of adult development theory: New ways of thinking about the life course* (pp. 87–95). San Francisco, CA: Jossey-Bass.

Tisdell, E. J. (2003). *Exploring spirituality and culture in adult and higher education*. San Francisco, CA: Jossey-Bass.

Tisdell, E. J. (2008). Spirituality and adult learning. In S. B. Merriam (Ed.), *New Directions for Adult and Continuing Education: No. 119. Third update on adult learning theory* (pp. 27–36). San Francisco, CA: Jossey-Bass.

United Methodist Communications. (2013). *Get real! Young adults have authenticity radar*. Retrieved from http://www.umcom.org/site/apps/nlnet/content3.aspx?c=mrLZJ9PFKmG&b=5262791&ct=13085241

Wuthnow, R. (2007). *After the baby boomers: How twenty- and thirty-somethings are shaping the future of American religion*. Princeton, NJ: Princeton University Press.

STEVEN B. FRYE *is an interim director and assistant professor in the School of Interdisciplinary Studies at Tennessee Technological University.*

6

*This chapter considers how transitions to adulthood have been histori-
cally represented and presents alternative ways of thinking about transitions to adulthood through the context of adult basic education programs.*

Youths Transitioning as Adult Learners

C. Amelia Davis

The U.S. Department of Education estimated the number of school leavers[1]
between the ages of 16 and 24 at about 3.0 million (Chapman, Laird, Ifill,
& KewalRamani, 2011), and the 2012 statistics reported by the GED Testing
Service showed that 59% of GED test takers in 2012 were between the ages
of 16 and 24 years old.[2] During the past 15 years, there has been a changing demographic in adult basic education due to an increase in the number
of traditional high school-aged students (ages 16–20) enrolled in Adult Basic
Education (ABE) and Adult Secondary Education (ASE; Hayes, 1999; Imel,
2003; Perin, Flugman, & Spiegel, 2006). Some explanations offered as reasons for this trend include (a) increased requirements for graduation due to
school reform measures (Hayes, 1999) and (b) the condition set forth in the
Adult Education and Family Literacy Act (Title II of the Workforce Investment
Act [WIA]) that stipulates *adult education* includes those "individuals who have
attained 16 years of age and who are not enrolled or required to enroll in secondary school under state law" (WIA, 1998, Title II, Section 203). It is the latter, the WIA inclusion of 16-year-olds into adult education, that is important
when considering the increase in 16- to 24-year-old students in ABE and GED
programs traditionally geared toward adult learners. These programs have now
become legitimate alternatives for youth in some states (Smith, 2002). This
makes it important for adult educators to consider the implications that youths
transitioning as adult learners might have on program planning and policy in
adult education.

The purpose of this chapter is to consider how transitions to adulthood
have been historically represented in the United States and to present alternative ways of thinking about transitions to adulthood through the context
of youth transitions as adult learners in adult education programs.[3] I begin
the chapter with a brief overview of transitions to adulthood and the historical context of adult basic education programs. Next, I present a commen-
tary on youths transitioning as adult learners that includes findings from a
recent narrative study in which 18- to 25-year-old GED students shared their

NEW DIRECTIONS FOR ADULT AND CONTINUING EDUCATION, no. 143, Fall 2014 © 2014 Wiley Periodicals, Inc.
Published online in Wiley Online Library (wileyonlinelibrary.com) • DOI: 10.1002/ace.20105

experiences transitioning from high school to adult education. Finally, I touch upon what can be learned from the historical and social context of transitions and the implications for adult education programming and policy.

Conceptualizing Transitions

In the United States, young people have been socialized by parents, school systems, and American media to follow a particular path, hitting certain benchmarks along the way to becoming an adult (Arnett, 2000; Furstenberg, Kennedy, McLoyd, Rumbaut, & Settersten, 2004; Rankin & Kenyon, 2008). Five historical markers have often been used to delineate the transition to adulthood: completing school, leaving home, beginning one's career, marrying, and becoming a parent (Settersten & Ray, 2010; Shanahan, Porfeli, & Mortimer, 2005; Waters, Carr, & Kefalas, 2011). The trouble is that these markers present a majoritarian, heteronormative discourse of adulthood and fail to take into account individuals from more diverse backgrounds who may or may not have the agency to hit those developmental markers in just the right order to signal entry into adulthood. These youths face different challenges during their transition to adulthood and they are often left with less agency than their middle-class counterparts, for example.

From a historical perspective, two major changes in the 20th century interfered with work and family life, thus shifting traditional views regarding entry into adulthood (Fussel & Furstenberg, 2005). First, technological innovation soared; "the workplace" was "the engine," changing the nature of adult education, and "technology" was "its fuel" (Rachal, 1989, p. 7). Attention was drawn to the workforce, the importance of technical education, and the need for increased technical training. Second, and perhaps more important, was the gender revolution, which "lowered barriers for women to enter the workplace" (Fussel & Furstenberg, 2005, p. 46). These two changes led to more men and women going to school, some for extended periods of time, to receive the training necessary to keep up with advancing technology. Because they were no longer tied to the home and motherhood, the gender revolution led women to prolong their transition to an adulthood that included taking on adult roles such as wife and mother. Now, there is less emphasis put on historical markers of adulthood, and youth are more active participants in constructing their own identities (Rankin & Kenyon, 2008).

Transitions are generally considered smooth for college-bound, middle-class youth, but research is limited for youth from other backgrounds (Osgood, Foster, & Courtney, 2010). These groups of youth are referred to as marginalized, vulnerable (Osgood et al., 2010), and disconnected (Waters et al., 2011). Despite what little is known about these groups, it is speculated that they struggle to navigate the transition to adulthood due to systemic inequities and access to resources (Jekielek & Brown, 2005). High school leavers could be identified as part of any of the groups mentioned above. Through their stories, we better understand the multiple layers involved in transitioning to adulthood, acknowledging the social and cultural factors often left out of these discussions.

Historical Overview of Adult Basic Education

In the 17th and 18th centuries, adult education took the form of apprenticeships and informal adult learning in homes, churches, taverns, and town meetings (Stubblefield & Keane, 1994). The history of adult education, however, has been "complicated by the changing idea about who is considered an adult" (Sticht, 2002, p. 4). For example, Long (1975) reported that age 14 was considered a marker for adulthood during early colonial times. When collecting information on adult literacy in the 1840, 1850, and 1860 census, the U.S. Census Bureau defined an adult as age 20 or over (Soltow & Stevens, 1981), yet in 1870, the definition of adult was changed to include persons 10 and older (Cook, 1977; Soltow & Stevens, 1981). From 1900 to 1940, the U.S. Census Bureau used people age 10 and older to calculate literacy statistics and age 14 and older from 1950 through 1970. Since 1970, age 16 or older has qualified as an adult for U.S. Census data statistics regarding adult basic education (Cook, 1977), and, as noted earlier, currently age 16 is identified under the Workforce Investment Act as the age at which individuals not enrolled in nor required to enroll in secondary school are eligible to receive adult education services. While age 16 is a marker of eligibility for adult education services, age 18 marks entry into legal adulthood in the United States as indicated by the right to legally work, participate in contracts, vote, marry, give sexual consent, and join the military ("Age of Majority," 2005). This contradiction between how an adult is defined in the United States and whom adult education includes causes confusion among adult educators, researchers, and students alike.

The Kennedy administration's War on Poverty in the 1960s served as an impetus for the current formal adult education system in the United States today. During that decade, education was beginning to be recognized as a means to improve the economic status of the poor and unemployed. In 1964, the signing of the Economic Opportunity Act (EOA) was a turning point for adult education, and Title II B marked the first time that federal funds were allocated for adult literacy education. The Adult Basic Education Program of Title II B required that adult basic education be provided for adults 18 years of age or older who had completed eight or fewer grades of schooling. Then, in 1970 with the Title II B amendments the Adult Education Act opened up to include Americans 16 years of age or older. When the inclusive age was lowered, the number of adults potentially affected and now eligible for adult education services rose from 24 million to 69 million (Cook, 1977).

In 1998, Title II of the WIA replaced the EOA of 1964. Like the welfare reform two years earlier, WIA shared a workforce development interest that would eventually affect Adult Basic Education. The 1998 WIA funding supported adult literacy programs in the United States and dictated that ABE

programs must assist (a) adults in becoming literate and obtaining the knowledge and skills necessary for employment and self-sufficiency, (b) adults who
are parents in obtaining the educational skills necessary to become full partners in the educational development of their children, and (c) adults in the
completion of secondary school education. As St. Clair and Belzer (2010) reminded readers, the WIA of 1998 impacted ABE as it consolidated workforce
development and ABE systems under one funding stream. The move of ABE
under the umbrella of workforce development allowed researchers, program
planners, and practitioners to form new partnerships that focused on the development of employability skills (St. Clair & Belzer, 2010).

Despite its complex history and minor successes, adult basic education
remains a field that transforms lives on a daily basis. Its impact is not to be
overlooked. It is important to remember that 93 million adults in the United
States struggle with literacy, 30 million have skills considered *below basic* literacy (Baer, Kutner, Sabatini, & White, 2009). According to the 2003 *National
Assessment of Adult Literacy (NAAL), below basic* is the lowest Basic Reading
Skills (BRS) level; adults at this level read fewer than 60 words correctly per
minute (White & Dillow, 2005). Lack of basic skills potentially affects an individual's ability to earn a living wage. Furthermore, many adults do not have the
literacy skills they need to help their children with school, to take better care of
their health and the health of their families, or to vote and participate fully in
civic life. Adult basic education is able to play a role in the lives of adults who
seek to improve their basic skills for both personal and professional growth.
Understanding the history of adult basic education since its formal inception
in 1964 is important in order to realize that over the years ABE has been a
means toward emancipation and economic stability. Youths transitioning as
adult learners are often seeking that emancipation in some form when they
enter the adult education classroom.

Youths Transitioning as Adult Learners

When considering transitions to adulthood for youths transitioning as adult
learners (from high school to adult education), it is necessary to consider the
markers traditionally identified with the path to adulthood, inaugural moments of adulthood, as well as structure and agency for youths transitioning
to adulthood. These should not be viewed independently, however, as they are
all interrelated. First, it should be noted that society influences the way age is
viewed by multiple groups; however, there are still perceptions about the appropriate ages at which life experiences should take place. So, despite the five
traditional markers used to delineate becoming an adult, adulthood is accelerated for some youths and delayed for some, depending upon circumstances,
structures, and agency.

Inaugural moments can be described as events marked by youth as their
entry into adulthood and perhaps consequential in nature, having implications for self-identity and often centered on responsibility, like parenthood and

caring for others (Davis, 2012). Inaugural moments are important because they provide a way to capture how social and economic environments frame individual experiences and the personal and cultural resources on which youths transitioning to adulthood are able to draw.

Structure and agency (Giddens, 1984) are always present, but it is important for adult educators to consider the structures facing youths transitioning as adult learners in order to best meet their needs. Structures like race, social class, and education can influence how and when people consider themselves to be adult. For example, low-income youth and emerging adults of color have been found to have an earlier sense of adulthood than White youth and emerging adults because they often grew up with more family responsibilities in childhood and adolescence (Fuligni, Tseng, & Lam, 1999). For this reason, social class, gender, race, education, and ethnicity structures are important in developing an understanding of transitions to adulthood because transitions are "structurally produced as well as culturally framed" (Quinn, 2010, p. 124).

A recent qualitative study by Davis (2012) explored the experiences of twelve 18- to 25-year-old GED students and their understanding of adulthood and their experiences about leaving high school and transitioning to adult education. Their narratives described race, class, and gender structures as having framed their transitions to adulthood, particularly as the structures related to accelerated adulthood. Two participants from Davis's study, Alan and Booman, African American males who identified as low-income and middle class, respectively, described how they shouldered responsibility for their siblings at an early age and how that responsibility made them feel like adults while still quite young themselves.

While caring for siblings is just one way two of Davis's (2012) male participants described feeling like an adult at an early age, one of the traditional five markers of adulthood includes becoming a parent; it is the last in the list of five presented by Shanahan et al. (2005). One third of teen girls who leave high school cite pregnancy or parenthood as the key reason (Shugar, 2012). However, having a baby as a teenager is likely not the marker of adulthood that was historically expected, and as a teen, having a baby can be a transforming event that challenges early adult development (Leadbeater & Way, 2001). Modell (1998) has suggested that young people without children are less likely to identify parenthood as an important marker or condition of adulthood, but those with children tend to view becoming a parent a marker of their own transition, implying that in becoming parents young people begin to view parenthood as a condition of adult status. In Davis's (2012) work, five participants identified as low-income, had children before the age of 20, and described becoming a parent as their pathway to adulthood. Though becoming a parent is not traditionally viewed as "necessary" for becoming an adult, Arnett (2003) found that emerging adults who had become parents often stated that "becoming a parent vaulted them suddenly and irrevocably into adulthood" (p. 73), reiterating that inaugural moments and nonnormative paths must be taken into consideration.

It is important to point out the systemic inequality that exists in the U.S. education system and how that inequality continues growing ever wide. Many adult basic education students view themselves as part of some sort of "underclass" with no opportunity for upward mobility. This is the rhetoric of neoliberal governments that suggest structures of race, class, and gender are giving way to personal choices when, in practice, social and cultural capital continue to be hindered by these inequalities (Holland & Thomson, 2009). For many youth in transition, there is agency in the decision to leave high school but that decision has consequences such as limited work and limited education opportunities. Such agentic moments have the potential to lead to greater personal and financial independence but for high school leavers, education and employment surface as the two main structures by which they are challenged. This is also an example of the duality of structure discussed by Giddens (1984). While there is agency in the decision to leave school, there is also constraint by the structures in place that limit mobility into and within the workforce. Enrolling in GED classes demonstrates personal agency that, in turn, leads to more agentic moments within existing or newly created structures. This is due to the fact that choices available after obtaining a GED have the potential to be less limited due to completion of what is considered to be equivalent to a high school diploma (Maralani, 2011).

With knowledge about the accelerated paths to adulthood, structures in place that limit agency for youths transitioning as adult learners, and perhaps even an understanding of the expectations—both personal and societal—that youths in adult education have or bring with them, adult educators can better serve this student population. There are implications for both programming and policy when considering youths in adult education programs and their transition to adulthood.

Implications for Adult Education

Rather than advocate for implications that make monumental shifts in the field, it is important to start local with the potential to address change gradually and with understanding. Young adults are what Knowles (1973) referred to as a "neglected species," and more time should be spent meeting their needs (Darkenwald & Knox, 1984, p. 100), particularly as those needs pertain to high school leavers. High school leavers are at an ever-increasing disadvantage (Smith, 2002) due to education and economic reforms and the continual stigma and stereotyping attached to not graduating from high school. In closing, I will discuss the implications for programming and practice and policy in meeting the needs of this population.

Programming and Practice. As Darkenwald and Knox (1984) proposed, an approach to program planning that is "comprehensive, responsive to their lifestyles, and takes multiple internal and external influences into account" has been known to be a successful approach for programs that serve younger adult learners (p. 102). GED classes appear to be a welcome change

New Directions for Adult and Continuing Education • DOI: 10.1002/ace

from traditional schooling for many youths transitioning as adult learners (Davis, 2012). Students feel more appreciated and are able to witness their own progress. This illustrates the need for programs to find ways to offer one-on-one learning experiences for students every day in the classroom from instructors who seem like they care, treat them differently than high school teachers, and do not use high school discipline in the adult education classroom. There is a call for adult education program planners and instructors to be sensitive to student stories, create a flexible learning environment, set clear expectations, provide relevant and appropriate curriculum for adult learners (Ambrose, Davis, & Ziegler, 2013), and be aware of resources available to students, particularly those students transitioning as adult learners and into adulthood (Davis, 2012; Xie, Sen, & Foster, Chapter 3 of this volume). Given limited funding and personnel in many adult education programs, community partnerships with social service offices, volunteer organizations, and even local universities or county school systems should be considered as one way to open spaces for collaboration and untapped resources for youths transitioning as adult learners.

Policy. It is not surprising that many high school leavers may not necessarily meet normative age markers of development in the order they were expected to meet them. More consideration should be given to the resources that are available for people who "hit those marks" at a younger age. The more important questions to ask may be, "What type of systems and services are in place for those youth? How can adult education and its connection to workforce development, social services, grant funding, and so on, create change?" This is a place where policy might intervene and focus on college recruitment and retention for this group (Maralani, 2011). Policy makers have recently focused their attention on programs designed for the early years in a child's life, just before he or she enters public school. I contend it is important to also offer services and support networks for youths who are in transition to an early adulthood, much like some of the participants in Davis's (2012) study. Social institutions and structures need to be refashioned to better reflect the changing nature of adulthood because "whether by choice or circumstance, adulthood no longer begins when adolescence ends" (Settersten & Ray, 2010, p. 36). First, social institutions and government agencies should acknowledge and address the lack of resources for those identified as "vulnerable populations." Once the lack of resources is addressed, as well as what resources are needed, services and programs can be implemented without age limitations and with integrated youth and adult systems.

Conclusions

The path to adulthood is not the same for all youth. In Western society there is "no single experience [that] renders one an adult" (Settersten, 2011, p. 189) just as "there is not a rite or event that signifies unambiguously that a younger person has attained adult status" (Arnett, 2003, p. 73). Instead, adulthood is situated within social, political, cultural, and historical structures and development cannot be generalized across race, social class, and educational level. As adult educators better understand how personal experiences such as school leaving and inaugural moments of adulthood influence development in youths transitioning as adult learners, they will better serve the changing demographic matriculating into adult basic education programs.

Notes

1. The term "dropout" was rendered in the 1960s and brought with it political, social, cultural, and economic interpretations (Anders, 2009; Dorn, 1993). In this chapter, the term "school leaver" replaces "dropout" to avoid negative connotations associated with the term "dropout" (Dorn, 1993).

2. Though it is not known how many of these students were enrolled in adult basic education and GED programs, it can be assumed that most were due to state and federal enrollment requirements prior to taking the GED test.

3. In this chapter, the terms adult basic education and GED are used interchangeably to refer to adult education programming under WIA.

References

Age of majority. (2005). In S. Phelps & J. Lehman (Eds.), *West's encyclopedia of American law* (2nd ed., Vol. 1, p. 166). Detroit, MI: Gale Virtual Reference Library.

Ambrose, V. K., Davis, C. A., & Ziegler, M. F. (2013). From research to practice: A framework for contextualized teaching and learning. *Journal of College Reading and Learning, 43*(3), 35–50.

Anders, A. D. (2009). Drop outs. In E. F. Provenzo (Ed.), *The encyclopedia of the social and cultural foundations of education* (pp. 261–265). Thousand Oaks, CA: Sage.

Arnett, J. J. (2000). Emerging adulthood: A theory of development from the late teens through the twenties. *American Psychologist, 55*(5), 469–480.

Arnett, J. J. (2003). Conceptions of the transition to adulthood among emerging adults in American ethnic groups. In J. J. Arnett & N. L. Galambos (Eds.), *New Directions for Child & Adolescent Development: No. 100. Exploring cultural conceptions of the transition to adulthood* (pp. 63–76). San Francisco, CA: Jossey-Bass.

Baer, J., Kutner, M., Sabatini, J., & White, S. (2009, February). *Basic reading skills and the literacy of America's least literate adults: Results from the 2003 National Assessment of Adult Literacy (NAAL)* (NCES 2009-481). Retrieved from http://nces.ed.gov/pubs2009/2009481.pdf

Chapman, C., Laird, J., Ifill, N., & KewalRamani, A. (2011). *Trends in high school dropout and completion rates in the United States: 1972–2009* (NCES 2012-006). U.S. Department of Education. Washington, DC: National Center for Education Statistics. Retrieved from http://nces.ed.gov/pubs2012/2012006.pdf

Cook, W. (1977). *Adult literacy education in the United States*. Newark, DE: International Reading Association.

Darkenwald, G. G., & Knox, A. B. (1984). Themes and issues in programming for young adults. In G. G. Darkenwald & A. B. Knox (Eds.), *New Directions for Adult and Continuing Education: No. 21. Meeting the educational needs of young adults* (pp. 99–105). San Francisco, CA: Jossey-Bass.

Davis, C. A. (2012). *The construction and performance of adulthood in 18- to 25-year-old GED students: A narrative exploration* (Doctoral dissertation). Retrieved from WorldCat Dissertations. (Accession No. OCLC: 810336124)

Dorn, S. (1993). Origins of the "dropout problem." *History of Education Quarterly, 33*(3), 353–373.

Fuligni, A. J., Tseng, V., & Lam, M. (1999). Attitudes toward family obligations among American adolescents with Asian, Latin American, and European backgrounds. *Child Development, 70*(4), 1030–1044.

Furstenberg, F., Kennedy, S., McLoyd, V. C., Rumbaut, R. G., & Settersten, R. A. (2004). Growing up is harder to do. *Contexts, 3*(3), 33–41.

Fussel, E., & Furstenberg, F. (2005). The transition to adulthood during the twentieth century: Race, nativity, and gender. In R. A. Settersten, F. Furstenberg, & R. G. Rumbaut (Eds.), *On the frontier of adulthood: Theory, research, and public policy* (pp. 29–75). Chicago, IL: The University of Chicago Press.

Giddens, A. (1984). *The constitution of society: Outline of the theory of structuration.* Cambridge, UK: Polity Press.

Hayes, E. (1999). Youth in adult literacy education programs. *Annual Review of Adult Learning and Literacy, 1*, 74–110.

Holland, J., & Thomson, R. (2009). Gaining perspective on choice and fate. *European Societies, 11*(3), 451–469.

Imel, S. (2003). Youth in adult basic and literacy education programs. *ERIC Digest No. 246.* Retrieved from http://www.calpro-online.org/eric/docs/dig246.pdf

Jekielek, S., & Brown, B. (2005, May). *The transition to adulthood: Characteristics of young adults ages 18 to 24 in America.* Washington, DC: The Annie E. Casey Foundation, Population Reference Bureau, and Child Trends.

Knowles, M. S. (1973). *The adult learner: A neglected species.* Houston, TX: Gulf Publishing Company.

Leadbeater, B. J. R., & Way, N. (2001). *Growing up fast: Transitions to early adulthood of inner-city adolescent mothers.* Mahwah, NJ: Lawrence Erlbaum Associates.

Long, H. B. (1975). Adult education in colonial America. *Journal of Research and Development in Education, 8*, 1–101.

Maralani, V. (2011). From GED to college: Age trajectories of nontraditional educational paths. *American Educational Research Journal, 48*(5), 1058–1090. doi: 10.3102/0002831211405836

Modell, J. (1998). Responsibility and self-respect: How alone do Americans stand? *Human Development, 41*, 316–320.

Osgood, D. W., Foster, E. M., & Courtney, M. E. (2010). Vulnerable populations and the transition to adulthood. *Transition to Adulthood, 20*(1), 209–229. Retrieved from http://www.futureofchildren.org/futureofchildren/publications/docs/20_01_10.pdf

Perin, D., Flugman, B., & Spiegel, S. (2006). Last chance gulch: Youth participation in urban adult basic education programs. *Adult Basic Education: An Interdisciplinary Journal for Adult Literacy Educational Planning, 16*(3), 171–188.

Quinn, J. (2010). Rethinking "failed transitions" to higher education. In K. Ecclestone, G. Biesta, & M. Hughes (Eds.), *Transitions and learning through the lifecourse* (pp. 118–129). London, UK: Routledge.

Rachal, J. R. (1989). The social context of adult and continuing education. In S. B. Merriam & P. Cunningham (Eds.), *Handbook of adult and continuing education* (pp. 3–14). San Francisco, CA: Jossey-Bass.

Rankin, L., & Kenyon, D. (2008). Demarcating role transitions as indicators of adulthood in the 21st century: Who are they? *Journal of Adult Development, 15*(2), 87–92.

Settersten, R. A. (2011). Becoming adult: Meaning and markers for young Americans. In M. C. Waters, P. J. Carr, M. Kefalas, & J. Holdaway (Eds.), *Coming of age in America: The transition to adulthood in the twenty-first century* (pp. 169–190). Berkley: University of California Press.

Settersten, R. A., & Ray, B. (2010). What's going on with young people today? The long and twisting path to adulthood. *Transition to Adulthood, 20*(1), 19–42. Retrieved from http://www.futureofchildren.org/futureofchildren/publications/journals/journal_details/index.xml?journalid=72

Shanahan, M. J., Porfeli, E., & Mortimer, J. T. (2005). Subjective age identity and the transition to adulthood: When does one become an adult? In R. A. Settersten, F. Furstenberg, & R. G. Rumbaut (Eds.), *On the frontier of adulthood: Theory, research and public policy* (pp. 225–255). Chicago, IL: University of Chicago Press.

Shugar, L. (2012). *Teen pregnancy and high school dropout: What communities can do to address these issues.* Washington, DC: The National Campaign to Prevent Teen and Unplanned Pregnancy and America's Promise Alliance. Retrieved from http://thenationalcampaign.org/resource/teen-pregnancy-and-high-school-dropout

Smith, H. (2002). The challenge of teens in the adult education classroom. *Literacy Links,* 6(4). Retrieved from http://www-tcall.tamu.edu/newsletr/jun02/jun02c.htm

Soltow, L., & Stevens, E. (1981). *The rise of literacy and the common school in the United States: A socioeconomic analysis to 1870.* Chicago, IL: University of Chicago Press.

St. Clair, R., & Belzer, A. (2010). Adult basic education. In C. E. Kasworm, A. D. Rose, & J. M. Ross-Gordon (Eds.), *Handbook of adult and continuing education* (pp. 189–197). Thousand Oaks, CA: Sage.

Sticht, T. G. (2002). The rise of the adult education and literacy system in the United States: 1600–2000. *The Annual Review of Adult Learning and Literacy,* 3(2), 1–26.

Stubblefield, H., & Keane, P. (1994). *Adult education in the American experience: From the colonial period to the present.* San Francisco, CA: Jossey-Bass.

Waters, M. C., Carr, P. J., & Kefalas, M. (2011). Introduction. In M. C. Waters, P. J. Carr, M. Kefalas, & J. Holdaway (Eds.), *Coming of age in America: The transition to adulthood in the twenty-first century* (pp. 1–27). Berkley: University of California Press.

White, S., & Dillow, S. (2005). *Key concepts and features of the 2003 National Assessment of Adult Literacy* (NCES 2006-471). U.S. Department of Education. Washington, DC: National Center for Education Statistics. Retrieved from http://nces.ed .gov/NAAL/PDF/2006471.PDF

Workforce Investment Act (WIA). (1998). *Title II adult education and literacy.* Retrieved from http://www.doleta.gov/usworkforce/wia/wialaw.pdf

C. AMELIA DAVIS is an assistant professor of educational research in the Department of Curriculum, Foundations, and Reading in the College of Education at Georgia Southern University.

New Directions for Adult and Continuing Education • DOI: 10.1002/ace

7

This chapter frames the transition to adulthood in the context of the moving from formal educational settings to the often less-structured learning that occurs in workplace settings. Although schooling may end, learning continues.

Transitions From Formal Education to the Workplace

Joann S. Olson

Any transition, by definition, involves moving away from one "place" and turning attention toward another. The elementary school student transitions to middle school. The transfer student leaves behind the community college and adjusts to life and learning in a university setting. The graduate leaves behind school and must become adept at learning on the job. It might be natural for the young adult transitioning from school to work to assume that he or she has been prepared for whatever is next. Yet, the forms of learning and evaluation prevalent in school settings (e.g., assignments, exams, and projects) are rarely central to workplace learning, where mastering one's responsibilities often requires a much less-structured route to acquiring necessary knowledge. New graduates encounter new modes of learning, new ways of being, and new settings for working, and they are often left feeling unprepared. This transition is, to borrow Settersten's (2005) phrase, "a blurry space" (p. 553). Therefore, helping young adults understand and navigate workplace learning is a key component of the transition to adulthood. This chapter highlights key aspects of the transition from school to work and suggests ways that adult educators can help young adults develop the skills they need as they leave the formal classroom and enter a rapidly changing workplace.

Leaving the Classroom

Given the many points at which an individual may make the shift from a primary focus on education to a focus on employment (e.g., dropping out or "stopping out" before graduation from high school or college, graduating with a high school diploma or college degree, completing graduate school), it is misleading to think of the school-to-work transition as something that is experienced in a consistent way from person to person. In fact, recent shifts

NEW DIRECTIONS FOR ADULT AND CONTINUING EDUCATION, no. 143, Fall 2014 © 2014 Wiley Periodicals, Inc.
Published online in Wiley Online Library (wileyonlinelibrary.com) • DOI: 10.1002/ace.20106

in the economy have also shifted the "traditional milestones of 'adulthood'" (Settersten & Ray, 2010, p. xii); it is no longer accurate to assume that graduation plus job equals financial (or residential) independence. However, across the literature, there are some common themes: feeling unprepared and encountering tension.

A Time of Feeling Unprepared. New graduates often describe a sense that something is missing or has been missed as they leave college and begin working. Martin, Matham, Case, and Fraser (2005) spoke with recent graduate chemical engineers, finding them "adequately, if not well, prepared to face the challenges of work in industry" (p. 178). At the same time, these graduates felt as though they had been "thrown into the deep end" on the job, unsure of what they should be doing, while also indicating that they "felt confident to tackle new problems and formulate a solution" (p. 178). They may have been adequately prepared, but they felt ill-equipped.

Farner and Brown (2008) noted that students did feel ready for the work world, but their data indicated that lower division students were more likely to feel confident than those closer to graduation. It is possible that the greater level of confidence expressed by younger students is misplaced, if the confidence is based on an inaccurate perception of their own abilities or the realities of what it takes to navigate the postcollege world; if this is the case, gaining a more realistic perspective before graduation is a positive outcome—even if it does result in lower levels of confidence in older students. Another possibility is that as upperclassmen near the end of their studies, they develop a sense of being unprepared for the postcollege world, and it is this sense of inadequacy that contributes to the lower confidence levels. Farner and Brown's study did not explore this aspect of preparedness, but the authors did suggest that the seeming mismatch in perceptions of work-readiness between potential employers and new entrants to the workforce could feed a sense of dissatisfaction on either side.

A Time of Tension. As Gardner and Lambert (1992) suggested, "being 'in college' has been a self-explanatory status and a laudatory one" (p. 4). Leaving school, however, brings a change in that status that often creates uncertainty. For college seniors in Yang and Gysbers's (2007) study, there was a relationship between decreased career search self-efficacy and increased psychological distress, suggesting that these students experience a "perceived lack of resources for the career transition" (p. 168). They also suggested that some students experience increased anxiety during this time—even if they feel ready for the transition—because they are aware of the potential risks inherent in the transition from college to work. One graduate described the transition as "a low time" (Perrone & Vickers, 2003, p. 69) and a "very uncomfortable kind of world" (p. 72).

Leaving school may also trigger changes in self-concept for which the young adult may or may not be prepared. The college-to-work transition can be a time when individuals make an "active investment" in developing identity and understanding "new meanings of career" (Stokes & Wyn, 2007, p. 495).

As Nyström, Dahlgren, and Dahlgren (2008) described, "graduates' vision and experiences of their professional trajectories do not seem to follow a specific temporal and logical progression in their career. Rather they appear in different order and at different points in time after graduation" (p. 215). In recent decades, the growing proportion of students who are "nontraditional" in some way—nearly 75% according to Chao, DeRocco, and Flynn (2007)—perhaps demonstrates this, as men and women evaluate current and future career options and determine that returning to school is the next best step for a desired career trajectory.

Holden and Hamblett (2007) followed college graduates for two years. Beyond themes of learning about the job, learning about the organization, and learning about self, they highlighted an underlying challenge. Participants expressed a desire to fully participate in their work community, which Holden and Hamblett called a desire for "cohesion" (p. 572). And yet, participants acknowledged that understanding the rules of their workplace would only begin once they failed in some way, labeled by Holden and Hamblett as "fragmentation" (p. 572). In other words, new graduates were seeking to connect and simultaneously realizing the connection might only occur after they had experienced a separation of sorts (i.e., failure). Likewise, Vaughan and Roberts (2007) described this as a time of both "security and exploration" (p. 91) when an individual's background (e.g., education, work experience, etc.) may strongly shape his or her approach to the options and the decisions encountered during this time of life.

Social class boundaries and norms may also play a role in the transition from school to work. Lubrano's (2004) interviews with "Straddlers"—men and women from blue-collar backgrounds who worked in white-collar settings—highlighted another set of challenges the young adult may face. Lubrano suggested that certain social norms are often necessary for success in a white-collar setting—navigating office politics, managing appropriate self-promotion, or networking, for example. For many young adults who are the first in their families to attend college or work in white-collar settings, these social skills may not have been part of their parents' work environment and, therefore, not part of the young adult's experience prior to engaging in the workforce. As one first-generation college graduate described her emerging understanding of the influence that workplace politics had on her work environment:

> My dad, he had politics [on his job], but a different kind of politics. You know, being working class, construction worker, I guess it would be, probably like a much cruder, more blatant version of what I go through. You know, just think about it, all these big, strapping, young to middle-aged [men], who work with their hands ... engaging in politics. It's a different game, but yet, it's probably some of the same rules. (Olson, 2010, p. 128)

Beyond being unfamiliar with some of these social moves, the young adult "Straddler" may actually find them distasteful or unethical: Lubrano (2004) suggested that the idea of networking may feel like a "dirty word" (p. 144) for those from blue-collar settings, as it contains an element of maneuvering relationships for personal gain. Even the new employee who "just came to do my job" (Olson, 2010, p. 128) will likely encounter interactions that do not make sense or norms that create internal (and possibly interpersonal) tension that the young adult is not able to fully articulate.

Preparing for an Unknown Future

In response to a rapidly changing world, several recent reports have high-lighted the necessity of developing "21st-century skills" in the rising work-force. A majority of employers (63%; Banerji, 2007) reported that "college graduates lack essential skills to succeed in today's global economy" (para. 1). These employers highlighted skills like teamwork in diverse groups, creativity, innovation, and critical or analytical reasoning as critical for success in an in-creasingly complex, multicultural economy. The definition of what comprises these "21st-century skills" varies. Gallup, Inc. (2013) used a list created by the Innovative Teaching and Learning Research project (collaboration, knowledge construction, problem solving and innovation, self-regulation, the use of tech-nology for learning, and skilled communication) as the basis for a recent sur-vey exploring the connection between these skills and quality of work life. Casner-Lotto and Barrington (2006) identified oral and written communica-tions, professionalism/work ethic, and critical thinking/problem solving as the "most important skills" (p. 7) for the 21st-century worker. Grit, tenacity, and perseverance topped the list of "critical factors for success in the 21st century" in a draft report released by the U.S. Department of Education (Shechtman, DeBarger, Dornsife, Rosier, & Yarnall, 2013). In at least one instance (Texas Higher Education Coordinating Board, n.d.), the regulatory body responsi-ble for state-level higher education policy is mandating changes to the core curriculum (i.e., general education requirements) that go beyond requiring "traditional" content-area core curriculum requirements, such as communi-cation, math, or science. Beginning in Fall 2014, Texas institutions of higher education must demonstrate that these courses also incorporate and promote the development of the following "21st-century competencies": critical think-ing skills, communication skills, empirical and quantitative skills, teamwork, social responsibility, and personal responsibility.

What employer *wouldn't* want a tenacious, professional, hard-working employee who could express herself clearly orally and in writing? What teacher *hasn't* hoped that his students were becoming collaborative, critical thinkers? And yet, with even the most cursory glance at these lists, the reader is bound to experience cognitive dissonance between these ideals and his or her expe-rienced reality. As revealed in Casner-Lotto and Barrington's (2006) report of employers' perceptions, more than half of high school graduates were deficient and only one in four college graduates were "perceived to be excellent" (p. 7) in these skills. Likewise, Gallup, Inc. (2013) reported that during their last year of school, only 22% of high school graduates and 27% of college graduates indicated that they had "often" applied what they were learning to real world problems (p. 10).

It is unclear how best to bridge the gap between what is provided and what is needed to better prepare graduates for this transition, particularly as calls for accountability, assessment, and demonstrated outcomes become increasingly central to educational policy. Dahlgren, Hult, Dahlgren, Segerstad, and Johannson (2006) suggested that a graduate's transition to work is shaped by the presence or absence of continuity between academic training and the type of employment he or she secured. Greater continuity allows for "immediate" (p. 583) socialization and accelerated acceptance into the professional community. Borden and Rajecki (2000), surveying those who had recently obtained a bachelor's degree in psychology, found that these graduates did not express a strong connection between the content of their classes and preparation for future employment. Borden and Rajecki further suggested that faculty and administrators who "take their responsibilities for guidance seriously" (p. 168) can help undergraduates develop appropriate expectations for postgraduation jobs. And yet, some graduates are left wondering what they gained by pursuing higher education. Coulon (2002) interviewed recent graduates in New Zealand who described themselves as "underemployed," and only 30% of those interviewed indicated that their current work "required graduate ability" (p. 293). In the current economic climate, which Settersten and Ray (2010) called a "do-it-yourself economy" (p. 53), where low-pay, low-prestige, service sector jobs are increasingly prevalent, college workshops, career coaching, or faculty mentoring may be an important first step. However, there are many paths along the transition to adulthood; it is unrealistic to aspire to completely preparing every student for every possible postgraduation outcome. Furthermore, the individual whose transition into the workforce does not involve a straight line from high school through college to career-level job may find very little in the way of resources or support for making their way.

Learning a New Kind of Learning

As mentioned elsewhere in this volume, the transition to adulthood is increasingly multidimensional and nonlinear, and the transition from school-based learning to workplace learning is equally complex. Facilitating this transition and helping young adults adjust to the new forms of learning they will encounter on the job requires more than a cursory nod to "what Millennials are like" or a seminar on intergenerational work relationships—although this information may be helpful (e.g., Lancaster & Stillman, 2010). Although men and women who finished college as nontraditional or adult learners may have previous work experiences to draw from, they also talk about the challenges of mastering a new work environment (Olson, 2011).

It is perhaps a cliché to declare that change is the only constant. Regardless, significant changes do occur during this stage of life. There are notable differences between the structured, formal learning environment and the informal learning that is standard in many work environments (Candy & Crebert, 1991), and this has perhaps become even more prevalent in the years since Candy and Crebert made this declaration. Etheridge (2007) identified "learning to think like a nurse" (p. 24) as a critical and important learning step for helping new graduate nurses learn to translate their skills and knowledge into proficiency when working in clinical settings for the first time. Brown (2004) described the decision making of recent graduates as "ongoing, iterative, and often nonlinear" (p. 377). As Candy and Crebert (1991) suggested, graduates can experience a "smooth passage" (p. 588) as they transition to work if they are aware of how the new environment may also shape their patterns and process of learning. At the risk of oversimplifying a complex and multifaceted issue, and recognizing that freedom and flexibility may be limited due to external constraints (i.e., accreditation or accountability issues) or budget limitations, several strategies may help educators who are working with young adults on both sides of this transition.

Highlight the Necessity of Noncognitive Skills. In studying the relationship between "21st-century skills" and work, Gallup, Inc. (2013) found that individuals who indicated having "often" participated in activities designed to develop these skills during their last year of school also reported higher work quality, in terms of having a role in decision making and being valued in the workplace. The Gallup, Inc. study did not elaborate on the nature of this relationship and, of course, it is not wise to speculate that the development of these skills *causes* higher work quality. However, if skills such as collaboration, problem solving, or communication are integral to the contemporary workplace, then it may be reasonable to conclude that individuals who have developed these skills are more likely to succeed. And indeed, initiatives such as the core curriculum requirements being implemented by the Texas Higher Education Coordinating Board (n.d.) are based on this conclusion; throughout the state, colleges and universities are being required to rewrite classes and revamp assessments to incorporate and develop these skills.

However, is it the impartation of these skills, or the student's *self-awareness* of these skills that reaps the real benefit? Are students aware of the efforts of educators and administrators to impart these skills? Educators may recognize the importance of developing professionalism in students and may incorporate classroom policies related to attendance and attention that are designed to impart these skills. However, as Weimer (2013) suggested, one of the biggest challenges facing educators is "convincing [students] that what happens in college classrooms is very similar to what happens in the world of work" (para. 4). Raising this awareness may be as simple as raising the visibility of the noncognitive aspirations of an assignment—including a statement that "this assignment is designed to develop your skill as a member of a team" or "this is a complex problem; be sure to address multiple approaches to the situation," for example. This approach may seem a bit obvious or pedantic to the educator, but for the student such links can serve as advance organizers between the required assignment and the anticipated outcome.

Noncognitive skills are, almost by definition, difficult to measure or assess. In addition, they do reveal and require a certain level of maturity, which the young adult may or may not have. Designing ad hoc workplace learning events around contemporary events or felt needs will likely increase engagement and participation. In addition, it may be critical for the educator in the workplace to help the young adult understand what is expected of them—especially in terms of these types of skills. A young adult who has been conditioned to expect that every team project will involve working together for a few hours over the course of a month with classmates he or she may never encounter again is almost certainly ill-prepared to manage team conflict on a long-term project. Taking the time to outline how "teamwork" or "collaboration" might work differently in the workplace from how it was experienced in the classroom will be time well invested in the young adult's transition to the workplace.

Incorporate "Real-World Realities" Into Assignments. The academic calendar is filled with new beginnings. There are ceremonies and seasons for new years, new semesters, new marking periods, new classes, new teachers, and new opportunities. There are mandated and predefined breaks every so often as well: teacher in-service days, semester breaks, even—in some places—time off for the opening day of deer season. Upon leaving school, the new entrant to the workforce, who has spent the majority of his or her life internalizing these cycles and seasons, suddenly encounters an environment where work is year-round, vacation time must be "earned" and "spent," and opportunities for a completely new start are few and far between. To be sure, these two environments are inherently different from one another. Schools will almost certainly always have marking periods, and most workplaces will not operate on an academic calendar. The young adult will need to navigate this change in culture and expectations.

The new entrant to the workforce also encounters a new reality: He or she may have very little control over the work that must be learned, mastered, and performed. There is immense value in helping learners develop autonomy and in allowing them to pursue learning projects that are interesting. And yet, by including a few more scripted assignments, such as requiring students to choose from a short list of project ideas or creating an assignment where one person starts a project and another must complete the project (picking up where the first student left off), the educator on the "school side" of the school-to-work transition can help prepare students for postschool realities. The contribution of these types of assignments to the student's eventual workplace learning can be maximized by challenging the student to engage in post-project self-reflection to articulate what was learned from the assignment and identify skills that were developed throughout the project.

Those on the "workplace learning" side of this transition also have a role to play. Young adults have spent the majority of their lives in educational settings where learning is something that can be measured against externally defined and imposed "standards." Therefore, the challenge facing the workplace educator is finding a way to help the young adult to identify work assignments and workplace interactions as a type of learning. Just as the classroom educator can help prepare students by imposing external constraints and structure onto assignments, the workplace educator can help facilitate this transition by creating benchmarks to help the young adult "measure" his or her progress and learning.

Recognizing a Complex Transition

Regardless of the level of schooling completed or the type of workplace encountered, the young adult is almost certainly managing change on multiple fronts—social, professional, economic, and so on. Furthermore, two individuals with the same degree from the same institution in similar entry-level jobs may have very different workplace learning needs, simply because one is a first-generation college graduate who finds the social aspects of his or her white-collar workplace perplexing, whereas the other developed an understanding of middle-class norms over the course of a lifetime. There is no one-size-fits-all program for helping young adults adjust to the realities of the workplace and the learning encountered therein. At the same time, conscientious educators—in the classroom and in the workplace alike—can facilitate this transition for young adults by intentionally creating learning experiences that are designed for the time of life where schooling may end in a society where learning must continue.

References

Banerji, S. (2007). Report: Employers say college graduates lack essential skills to succeed in today's global economy. *Diverse: Issues in Higher Education, 23*(26), 18. Retrieved from http://diverseeducation.com/article/6979/

Borden, V. M. H., & Rajecki, D. W. (2000). First-year employment outcomes of psychology baccalaureates: Relatedness, preparedness, and prospects. *Teaching of Psychology, 27*(3), 164–168.

Brown, S. C. (2004). Where this path may lead: Understanding career decision-making for postcollege life. *Journal of College Student Development, 45*(4), 375–390.

Candy, P. C., & Crebert, R. G. (1991). Ivory tower to concrete jungle: The difficult transition from the academy to the workplace as learning environments. *The Journal of Higher Education, 62*(5), 570–592.

Casner-Lotto, J., & Barrington, L. (2006). *Are they really ready to work? Employers' perspectives on the basic knowledge and applied skills of new entrants to the 21st century U.S. workforce.* New York, NY: The Conference Board. Retrieved from http://www.p21.org/storage /documents/FINAL_REPORT_PDF09-29-06.pdf

Chao, E. L., DeRocco, E. S., & Flynn, M. K. (2007). *Adult learners in higher education: Barriers to success and strategies to improve results* (Occasional Paper No. 2007-03). Washington DC: U.S. Department of Labor, Employment and Training Administration.

Coulon, A. (2002). Underemployment amongst New Zealand graduates: Reflections from the lived experience. *New Zealand Journal of Industrial Relations, 27*(3), 283–297.

Dahlgren, M. A., Hult, H., Dahlgren, L. O., Segerstad, H. H., & Johannson, K. (2006). From senior student to novice worker: Learning trajectories in political science, psychology and mechanical engineering. *Studies in Higher Education, 31*(5), 569–586.

Etheridge, S. (2007). Learning to think like a nurse: Stories from new nurse graduates. *The Journal of Continuing Education in Nursing, 38*(1), 24–30.

Farner, S. M., & Brown, E. E. (2008). College students and the work world. *Journal of Employment Counseling, 45*, 106–114.

Gallup, Inc. (2013). *21st century skills and the workplace: A 2013 Microsoft Partners in Learning and Pearson Foundation study.* Washington, DC: Author. Retrieved from http://www.gallup.com/strategicconsulting/162821/21st-century-skills-workplace.aspx

Gardner, P. D., & Lambert, S. (1992). *It's a hard, hard, hard, hard world!* East Lansing: Michigan State University Career Development and Placement Services. Retrieved from ERIC database. (ED368997)

Holden, R., & Hamblett, J. (2007). The transition from higher education into work: Tales of cohesion and fragmentation. *Education & Training, 49*(7), 516–585.

Lancaster, L. C., & Stillman, D. (2010). *The M-factor: How the millennial generation is rocking the workplace.* New York, NY: Harper Business.

Lubrano, A. (2004). *Limbo: Blue-collar roots, white-collar dreams.* Hoboken, NJ: Wiley.

Martin, R., Matham, B., Case, J., & Fraser, D. (2005). Engineering graduates' perceptions of how well they were prepared for work in industry. *European Journal of Engineering Education, 30*(2), 167–180.

Nyström, S., Dahlgren, M. A., & Dahlgren, L. O. (2008). A winding road—professional trajectories from higher education to working life: A case study of political science and psychology graduates. *Studies in Continuing Education, 30*(3), 215–229.

Olson, J. S. (2010). *Chasing a passion: The early-career lived experience of first-generation college graduates* (Doctoral dissertation). Retrieved from ProQuest. (Accession Order No. AAT 3436090)

Olson, J. S. (2011, May). *"Back to the real world": First-generation adult graduates and the college-to-work transition.* Paper presented at the CCCU Center for Research in Adult Learning Annual Conference, Indianapolis, IN.

Perrone, L., & Vickers, M. H. (2003). Life after graduation as a 'very uncomfortable world': An Australian case study. *Education & Training, 45*(2), 69–78.

Settersten, R. A., Jr. (2005). Social policy and the transition to adulthood: Toward stronger institutions and individual capacities. In R. A. Settersten, Jr., F. F. Furstenberg, Jr., & R. G. Rumbaut (Eds.), *On the frontier of adulthood: Theory, research, and public policy* (pp. 534–560). Chicago, IL: The University of Chicago Press.

Settersten, R., & Ray, B. E. (2010). *Not quite adults: Why 20-somethings are choosing a slower path to adulthood, and why it's good for everyone.* New York, NY: Bantam Books Trade Paperbacks.

Shechtman, N., DeBarger, A. H., Dornsife, C., Rosier, S., & Yarnall, L. (2013). *Promoting grit, tenacity, and perseverance: Critical factors for success in the 21st century.* Washington, DC: U.S. Department of Education, Office of Educational Technology. Retrieved from http://www.ed.gov/edblogs/technology/files/2013/02/OET-Draft-Grit-Report-2-17-13.pdf

Stokes, H., & Wyn, J. (2007). Constructing identities and making careers: Young people's perspectives on work and learning. *International Journal of Lifelong Education, 26*(3), 495–511.

Texas Higher Education Coordinating Board. (n.d.). *Texas core curriculum.* Retrieved from http://www.thecb.state.tx.us/index.cfm?objectid=6AB82E4B-C31F-E344-C78E368852 4B44FB

Vaughan, K., & Roberts, J. (2007). Developing a 'productive' account of young people's transition perspective. *Journal of Education and Work, 20*(2), 91–105.

Weimer, M. (2013, August 7). Helping students learn to be professional [Blog post]. Retrieved from http://www.facultyfocus.com/articles/teaching-professor-blog/helping-students-learn-to-be-professional/

Yang, E., & Gysbers, N. C. (2007). Career transitions of college seniors. *The Career Development Quarterly*, *56*, 157–170. Retrieved from http://ncda.org/aws/NCDA/pt/sp/cdquarterly

JOANN S. OLSON *is an assistant professor and program coordinator in the adult and higher education program at the University of Houston-Victoria.*

New Directions for Adult and Continuing Education • DOI: 10.1002/ace

8

In this final chapter, we highlight recurring themes from the preceding chapters and discuss the potential impact these themes have on program planning and instructional practice in adult education.

Themes and Issues in Programming for Young Adults

Joann S. Olson, C. Amelia Davis

When Darkenwald and Knox (1984) drew upon Knowles's work to ask the question, "Are *young adults* a neglected species?" (p. 100)—and subsequently answered in the affirmative—we believe they were on to something. However, for 30 years young adults received little attention in the adult education literature. In this volume, we have aspired to reorient adult educators to young adults and update the discussion among adult educators regarding younger learners and their educational needs as they transition to adulthood. The previous chapters in this volume present a collage of approaches and issues to consider regarding the transitional needs of young adult learners. Despite the diversity of topics covered, a few recurrent themes are worth noting. In this final chapter, we will discuss those themes and the potential impact they have on program planning and instructional practice in adult education. We begin with the ambiguity of *transition*, followed by the complexity of contemporary society, young adults' need for belonging and community, and finally, the need for future research regarding young adults.

Ambiguity of Transition

Throughout this volume, the word *transition* has been conceptualized and constructed in multiple ways, demonstrating how the meaning it takes on is based on the social and cultural context in which it is used. There is ambiguity in the lexical choice of *transition*, and as Wyn illustrates in Chapter 1 through a historical account of youth transitions, there is ambiguity in the traditional metaphor of transition from youth to adult.

In traditional psychology, the term transition is used to refer to changes in behavior or cognition, whereas in developmental psychology, transition most often refers to movement from one stage of development to another. Sociologists attend to sociocultural relationships and define a transition as it relates to

NEW DIRECTIONS FOR ADULT AND CONTINUING EDUCATION, no. 143, Fall 2014 © 2014 Wiley Periodicals, Inc.
Published online in Wiley Online Library (wileyonlinelibrary.com) • DOI: 10.1002/ace.20107

shifts in identities, roles, and statuses. Considering more specifically the move from youth to adulthood, transition is often defined as a trajectory from dependence to independence. Osgood, Foster, and Courtney (2010) described the time between high school and the twenties as "a time of semi-autonomy during which youth typically remain dependent on their parents in many ways" (p. 210). It is a complex process in which youths, who have been dependents their entire lives, begin to move toward social independence and take on what are constructed as adult roles: citizen, spouse, parent, and worker (Waters, Carr, & Kefalas, 2011). However, how youths fare during their transition to adulthood can have long-term effects.

As Xie, Sen, and Foster point out in Chapter 3 of this volume, transitions are generally considered smooth for college-bound, middle-class youths, but research is limited for youths from other backgrounds. These groups of youth are referred to as marginalized, vulnerable, and disconnected (Osgood et al., 2010). Despite what little is known about these groups, it seems that they struggle to navigate the transition to adulthood due to systemic inequities and access to resources. When considering the transition from youth to adult, Wyn notes in Chapter 1 of this volume that there are gaps in our understanding related to the experiences of young people and the policies that inform program design and institutional planning.

Using the term *transition* implies that there is a simple and synchronous move from "youth" to "adult," an assumption that often minimizes the complexities and multiple transitions involved. Wyn reminds us in Chapter 1 that the traditional metaphor, "transition to adulthood," connotes that adulthood is a clearly defined status at which one arrives, drawing upon the idea that there is but one transition to a universally experienced adulthood. As the various chapters in this volume note, the life course is culturally and socially scripted, whether for young adults labeled with dis/abilities (Lester, Chapter 4), young adults seeking to make sense of their own cultural identity (Drayton, Chapter 2), young adults coming to understand themselves in a community of faith (Frye, Chapter 5), young adults taking nontraditional education routes (Davis, Chapter 6), young adults with earlier life histories that leave them vulnerable in some way (Xie et al., Chapter 3), or young adults setting out into the workplace for the first time (Olson, Chapter 7), illustrating that transitions are ambiguous and structured by economic and social resources.

This ambiguity of transition should be noted and acknowledged when working with young adults in adult education programs. Program planners and practitioners need to understand this ambiguity in order to connect with students in multiple ways in a variety of contexts when serving younger adult learners. In addition, the ambiguity of the transition to adulthood calls for practitioners to be reflexive and consider their own understanding of transition and their own understanding of adulthood. It is through this lens that they view and serve their young adult students. Acknowledging their own position can provide practitioners with the opportunity to open up to new

New Directions for Adult and Continuing Education • DOI: 10.1002/ace

understandings that may facilitate a more inclusive learning environment for young adult students.

Complexity of Contemporary Society

It is easy to resort to cliché, when talking about the pace of current society or the rapidly changing world that today's young adults encounter. Terms like "globalization" or "digital native" or even "Millennial" have been overused, perhaps to the detriment of deep understanding of these societal phenomena. However, the prevalence of these ideas in both popular and academic venues does highlight the reality that adult educators are preparing today's young adults for an unknown future in a complex society. The authors in this volume have highlighted various aspects of this complexity.

Clichés aside, the society we inhabit as adults, which young adults are learning to navigate, shapes much of our experience of adulthood. As Drayton suggests in Chapter 2 of this volume, though individuals in monocultural societies may not need to focus on or explore ethnic identity, making one's way in multicultural societies requires coming to terms with the racial, ethnic, cultural, and subcultural forces that have formed and will continue to form the young adult's sense of self. In Chapter 7 of this volume, Olson highlights that the notion of what it means to be "ready for the workplace" is shifting, as employers grow in their understanding of what it takes for an organization to be successful in the current economic environment.

In light of this, the authors here also challenge us to examine the terminology and labels that we use, to reflect more accurately the variations of experience made possible in contemporary society. Lester (Chapter 4 of this volume) seeks to add complexity and nuance to our understanding of the experience of young adults with dis/ability labels, even questioning the very nature of such labels. In Chapter 1 of this volume, Wyn goes so far as to challenge our use of the word *transition*, suggesting that it may be a relic of an earlier understanding of human experience and development, bound in a rhetoric of trajectories that no longer represent contemporary society or experience.

The experiential and educational pathways to adulthood are increasingly varied, as well. Xie et al. (Chapter 3 of this volume) highlight the challenges facing vulnerable youth, suggesting that not only is "the system" that exists for supporting these youth inefficient when these individuals are young, but also these supports are often removed abruptly, resulting in a jarring encounter with uncertainty and complexity. In adult education, our students often bring a complex set of experiences and expectations to their learning as well, as Davis (Chapter 6 of this volume) reminds us. Frye suggests, in Chapter 5 of this volume, that faith communities are also grappling with the ramifications of an increasingly multicultural and pluralistic society; those that fail will find their congregations aging and their numbers dwindling.

Considering the complexity of contemporary society, what role can adult educators play as young adult learners navigate their way toward adulthood?

First, we can strive to create learning environments that foster the development of young adult learners by cultivating awareness of the issues and challenges they face. Second, we can model ongoing exploration and investigation, igniting curiosity in students as Lang (2014) suggests and helping them formulate a natural interest for what is to come. Finally, we can demonstrate support and provide guidance. A little encouragement can go a long way. When adult educators work with young adults to become leaders of their own life journey, we have the potential to begin to meet their transitional needs in today's complex world.

Belonging and Community

In many cases, young adult learners are either currently experiencing or anticipating a time of significant change. As the authors here have sought ways to more effectively serve young adult learners, many have highlighted the importance of relationships as young adults navigate this transition. This idea of belonging and community runs through several of the chapters in this volume.

In Chapter 1, Wyn presents a research-driven challenge to how we conceptualize young adulthood and the transition to adulthood, suggesting that young adults actively seek meaningful connections to the various environments and relationships in their lives. She suggests that this work of "belonging" is perhaps the work of understanding and inhabiting adulthood. Furthermore, Drayton (Chapter 2) highlights young adulthood as a time of deciding and determining the extent to which one's culture and racial/ethnic identity of origin will be incorporated into one's own identity—in other words, where does the young adult belong, in relation to the groups and identities and relationships that were significant and formational from an early age?

In addition to the internally driven sense of belonging or community as described above, the authors also highlight other aspects of belonging and community. Externally ascribed labels or communities can significantly affect the experience of young adults, as highlighted in Lester's discussion of young adults with dis/ability labels (Chapter 4) or the experiences of "vulnerable youth" described by Xie et al. in Chapter 3. In Chapter 5, Frye discusses the double-sided nature of belonging: not only is the young adult seeking to belong, the community must be willing to accept and incorporate for that belonging to happen. Perhaps at the core of Olson's suggestions (Chapter 7) is the sense that many new entrants to the workforce find it challenging to adjust to the workplace when they have not yet learned what it takes to "belong" in the new setting.

Granted, *belonging* and *community* are slippery words, difficult to define. It is also likely that these are not things that can be directly taught. For adult educators seeking to meet the needs of young adult learners, these ideas can provide a helpful lens for understanding the varied experiences of those students.

New Directions for Adult and Continuing Education • DOI: 10.1002/ace

The Need for Future Research

The chapters in this volume bring together an interdisciplinary perspective on meeting the transitional needs of young adult learners. While this volume provides a good starting point for considering what it means to conceptualize transitions in a new way and to reconsider the ways in which adult educators work with young adults, it is by no means comprehensive and indicates the direct need for more research in the areas of young adults and their transitions to adulthood, particularly as related to adult education.

This volume reveals the needs for future research that will promote deeper understanding of the lived experiences of adult education students, marginalized youths, and their transitions to adult education and then to higher education and the workforce. For example, Lester notes in Chapter 4 that within the field of adult education dis/ability is not positioned as socially or culturally bound, indicating a gap that adult educators may want to consider filling by collaborating with scholars in the field of dis/ability studies. Similarly, Davis suggests in Chapter 6 that there is a need for more research regarding the transition from high school to adult education. Research that captures this transition from the student perspective is important for program administrators who want to learn more about what works with enrollment and retention.

As Xie et al. delineate in Chapter 3, recent neoliberal agendas and globalization necessitate a call for more critical studies of marginalized adult education student populations that focus on the impact of cultural institutions to legitimize certain ideologies, productions of knowledge, and social formations such as low-skilled labor. Drayton reminds us in Chapter 2 that it is important to question whether these political and cultural agendas have the potential to impact adult student development because they are built to maintain the existing class, race, and gender structures of society.

Like Olson's chapter (Chapter 7), many of the more recent discussions in adult education have focused on transitioning adult learners to the workforce or, less often, into higher education. The discussions about adult education have also focused on systemic and institutional practices of adult transitions rather than on the social practices of transitioning to adulthood. The next step is to initiate more interdisciplinary collaboration around the topics of transitions to adulthood. Collaboration can be a powerful tool in disseminating information to the largest audience. Though each field mentioned above may take a different approach to research, they have common interests and overlapping stakes in the potential findings of such efforts.

Summary

It will be no surprise to adult educators that the authors in this volume have highlighted the importance of presenting relevant content in an engaging, responsible, and reflective way. Every student brings his or her story to every learning setting; those stories are rich, they are messy, and they are important.

Adult educators in this complex society must reckon with those stories—for the benefit of the student.

Before 1998, the word "googol" was known by only those familiar with advanced mathematics; in our contemporary lexicon, "Google" has become ubiquitous—practically synonymous with "search"—to the extent that the word from which it was derived now looks like a misspelling. We inhabit a complex and ever-changing society, as this simple example demonstrates and as the contributors to this volume have described. Therefore, to Wyn's suggestion that we move from a metaphor of transition to a metaphor of belonging, we would add a challenge. Are we adequately equipping young adult learners for what they will need to become to meet the challenges that we cannot even imagine? This is an important conversation, and it should be ongoing. Let us not wait another 30 years to continue this discussion.

References

Darkenwald, G. G., & Knox, A. B. (Eds.). (1984). *New Directions for Adult and Continuing Education: No. 21. Meeting educational needs of young adults.* San Francisco, CA: Jossey-Bass.

Lang, J. M. (2014, January 22). Enough with the "lifelong learning" already: That tired phrase accomplishes little and means even less [Blog post]. Retrieved from http://chronicle.com/article/Enough-With-the-Lifelong/144137

Osgood, D. W., Foster, E. M., & Courtney, M. E. (2010). Vulnerable populations and the transition to adulthood. *Transition to Adulthood, 20*(1), 209–229.

Waters, M. C., Carr, P. J., & Kefalas, M. (2011). Introduction. In M. C. Waters, P. J. Carr, M. Kefalas, & J. Holdaway (Eds.), *Coming of age in America: The transition to adulthood in the twenty-first century* (pp. 1–27). Berkley: University of California Press.

JOANN S. OLSON *is an assistant professor and program coordinator in the adult and higher education program at the University of Houston-Victoria.*

C. AMELIA DAVIS *is an assistant professor of educational research in the Department of Curriculum, Foundations, and Reading in the College of Education at Georgia Southern University.*

New Directions for Adult and Continuing Education • DOI: 10.1002/ace

INDEX

Xie, R., 2, 29, 38, 69, 84, 85, 86, 87

Yang, E., 74
Yarnall, L., 76
You Lost Me, 54
Young adults, transition to adulthood, 63–70; and acculturation, 22–24; ambiguity of, 83–85; characteristics of, 6; conceptualization of, 64–65; culture and, 19–21; historical overview of, 65–66; implications of, for adult education, 68–69; metaphor of, 9–10; paths of, 66–68; social condition and, 19–21; theories of, 5–8

Youth with dis/ability labels, transition of, 39–47: adult education and, 44–45; allies, 46–47; competence, assumption of, 46; full-time employment and, 40–41; key policies supporting, 41–42, 42t; literature review on, 42–44; in National Longitudinal Study-2, 40; resources for supporting, 43t; social-relational model of dis/ability, 45; support to, 45–47; in United States, 40–41
Yovanoff, P., 31

Zamboanga, B., 19
Ziegler, M. F., 69
Zima, B. T., 31

delivering adult education programs through distance and online learning are undergoing continuous transformation by novel information technologies. Within institutions, CE units are increasingly collaborating with academic departments. In addition, demographic shifts have resulted in new audiences and types of programs offered, both credit and noncredit. Schools, especially state-supported ones, have been pressured to increase their participation in economic development. All these changes carry administrative considerations. This volume suggests perspectives and solutions for the challenges that must be successfully confronted by today's CE programs and the professionals who develop them.

ISBN: 978-1-1188-3487-9

ACE139 Decentering the Ivory Tower of Academia

Dianne Ramdeholl

For many, the academy has historically represented privilege and intellectual exclusion (primarily Eurocentric, White, and male); for others it has represented an increasingly contested site, as marginalized populations have challenged the myth of the ivory tower being a haven of meritocracy and equal opportunities. Still others persist in viewing universities as a level playing field, a place where people are judged primarily by their ideas and intellectual contributions.

Ironically, alongside these charged conversations of exclusivity, privilege, and opportunity has occurred the seduction of the ivory tower by market interests, sacrificing standards in the interests of ill-defined efficiency. Much has been written on the increasingly market-driven culture of higher education; many have called this commodification and instrumentalization the most dangerous ideology of the current historical moment.

Yet, within this landscape, there have been scholars willing to make space to critically interrogate higher education in relation to multiple systems of oppression. They are working to introduce new perspectives, nurturing counter-hegemonic knowledges. Many have struggled to cocreate and sustain democratic spheres that decenter dominant interests, with the aim of a more equitable society. They have been part of a larger movement of academic warriors, academics with consciences who live out their commitments by subscribing to the notion that scholarship and activism are inextricably inter-twined. This volume embodies their narratives and issues an open invitation.

ISBN: 978-1-1187-7109-9